I0128322

LAND OF OPPORTUNITY

LAND OF OPPORTUNITY

Immigrant Experiences in the
North American Landscape

Edited by Ruth McKoy Lowery,
Rose M. Pringle,
and Mary Ellen Oslick

ROWMAN & LITTLEFIELD
Lanham • Boulder • New York • London

Published by Rowman & Littlefield
An imprint of The Rowman & Littlefield Publishing Group, Inc.
4501 Forbes Boulevard, Suite 200, Lanham, Maryland 20706
www.rowman.com

6 Tinworth Street, London SE11 5AL

Copyright © 2019 by Ruth McKoy Lowery, Rose M. Pringle,
and Mary Ellen Oslick

All rights reserved. No part of this book may be reproduced in any form or by
any electronic or mechanical means, including information storage and retrieval
systems, without written permission from the publisher, except by a reviewer
who may quote passages in a review.

British Library Cataloguing in Publication Information Available

Library of Congress Cataloging-in-Publication Data Available

ISBN: 978-1-4758-4738-3 (cloth)
ISBN: 978-1-4758-4739-0 (pbk.)
ISBN: 978-1-4758-4743-7 (electronic)

Dedication

Ruth: For my brothers and sisters, and their families; immigrants who have actualized the American dream. And for our mother, Albertha McKoy, who made that dream possible!

Rose: To my mother, Melvie Brown-Johnson who taught her children how to work through adversities and embrace them as opportunities for mobility.

Mary Ellen: For those who shared their stories in this book—we all need to hear you.

CONTENTS

ACKNOWLEDGMENTS

This elevation of the authentic voices of immigrants in this professional contribution would not have been possible without the priceless support from our families, friends, and colleagues. A special thank you to Tom Koerner, whose faith in the project and encouragement kept us focused; and to the Rowman & Littlefield editorial and production teams, especially Carlie Wall and Hannah Fisher for their guidance throughout the development of the project.

We thank the reviewers whose constructive feedback helped to make this project a reality. Your insights, thoughtfulness, and critical suggestions are deeply appreciated. To Dr. Christian Faltis, thank you for devoting the time to write the foreword. You realized the vision and the volume's potential and immediately agreed to be a part of the project.

A book is nothing without the dedication of its authors; thus, we thank all the contributors who heeded the call to share their stories, worked diligently on their chapters, and responded in a timely manner to editorial reminders to bring this project to completion. Additionally, we wish to thank Dr. Evie Freeman and Dr. Terrell Young for agreeing to review the manuscript and write endorsements for this book at short notice.

LIST OF FIGURES

FOREWORD

Christian J. Faltis

Immigrants, refugees, and dispossessed persons and families represent a significant number of residents and community members across the United States. More importantly, these community members have children and youth who attend schools, churches, mosques, and synagogues, and most are employed in places where they are in daily contact with the public. More than one-fifth of our nation's children grow up in immigrant homes (Suárez-Orosco, Todorova, and Louie 2005).

In many large cities, immigrants and dispossessed families represent the largest communities of color. In others, immigrants and dispossessed families live side by side with African American and Mexican American families, many of whom are what John Ogbu, a Nigerian immigrant scholar (1939–2003), refers to as *involuntary minorities*, people who find themselves in the United States against their will, either through slavery trade or colonial annexation (Ogbu 1987).

Other minoritized peoples have been migrating continuously to and from what is now called the United States for centuries, well before the establishment of the United States and well before the colonial annexation of the central, southern, southwestern, and western regions of the United States through wars, purchases, and the extermination of indigenous peoples by the so-called pioneers. Others are relatively more recent, mainly as a result of changes in policy at the highest levels toward immigration by people of color from non-White European countries and continents.

For example, Chinese were singled out in 1882 until the 1960s as people who were not permitted to immigrate to the United States. In the early 1920s, non-White European immigrants from Eastern and Southern Europe were not welcomed; they were often denounced for destabilizing the English language and for cultural practices different from White, Protestant pioneers. Western European families considered Jews, gypsies, Slavic peoples, and Italians ignorant and lazy, shifty and untrustworthy. In recent decades, White Cubans were welcomed while Haitian refugees were not.

But, make no mistake about it, for the vast majority of White Americans, immigrants from non-White countries are problematic, especially in current times. "They are taking our jobs!" "They are rapists and drug dealers," "They don't pay taxes!" "They are ruining English," "They are cheating the welfare system," and "They are ruining our schools." Sadly enough, the anti-immigrant, anti-refugee rhetoric, which I refer to as the *distribution of disdain* (Faltis 2012), is extremely high among many Americans, and sadly, even among those whose family members were likely immigrants from non-White Western European countries that are now considered to be White.

This distribution of disdain motivated by fear of non-White proliferation by White communities can be seen throughout society in health, welfare, and schooling. Most recently, the distribution of disdain has fueled the mass incarceration of undocumented Mexican immigrants, their deportation and, most sorrowfully, the separation of children from their parents. Separating children from their parents and incarcerating them has been most likely to occur with Mexican and Central American families but also with Black Dominican and Haitian families (Suárez-Orosco et al. 2005).

THE ROLE OF EDUCATION

At the policy level, education in the United States has never favored positive solutions for addressing the language, social, and learning needs of immigrant children and youth who attend U.S. schools. The United States has a long history of segregation and, more recently, hyper-segregation of immigrant children and youth to keep them in separate settings within school buildings (Gifford and Valdés 2006). Immigrant children and youth, particularly recent arrivals with minimal or no prior schooling in English, or, in some cases, minimal or interrupted educational experiences, are often immediately physically separated and linguistically isolated from others for up to two years before gaining access to and participating in mainstream classes (Faltis and Arias 2007). These students are labeled: called English learners (rather than recognizing their bilingualism) and other terms (e.g., Limited English Proficient) that may be extended to infer intellectual inferiorities and deficits.

Immigrant students fortunate enough to enter strong bilingual and dual language programs where they learn literacy practices and other content in their home languages have a much better chance of adjusting and adapting healthily to the school communities. They can also selectively sustain cultural practices that build strong social and cultural identities, provided the programs are well-designed, culturally sustaining, and long enough for students to develop bilingually and with biliteracy in their home language as they also learn in and through English.

Most immigrant children and children of dispossessed families are provided only with English as a second language support, typically in a separate program, or they are pulled out of class for a part of their school day to work with an English-as-a-second-language teacher. Their languages and cultural practices are not invited or integrated into the school curriculum or community.

CULTURALLY RESPONSIVE AND CULTURALLY SUSTAINING TEACHING

One of the few areas in education where teachers and scholars have been successful with immigrant children and children of dispossessed families is when they incorporate culturally responsive and culturally sustaining pedagogies. I won't use space here to define these important pedagogies because this is the main topic of this volume. As authors in this volume point out, in multiple ways, culturally responsive and sustaining pedagogies leverage the cultural and political funds of knowledge, language uses, and cultural practices that immigrant children and children of dispossessed families bring with them to school to make classrooms and schools more inviting.

These pedagogies allow for more politically attuned awareness and ultimately more engagement with these children and their families. Being a culturally responsive building principal, secretary, counselor, teacher, and teacher's aide means that these critical actors in schools have prepared themselves to disrupt deficit thinking about immigrant children and children of dispossessed families. They interact with and ultimately teach children in ways that draw on the language and cultural practices of the children and communities they serve, and they do so in ways that go against the grain of curriculum and schooling that was set up to privilege monolingual, middle-class White students.

As the authors in this volume make clear, there is so much to learn about children from indigenous cultures (both native and immigrant indigenous peoples). People from Saudi and Arab cultures, from Somali and Nepalese cultures, from Filipino American cultures, from Chinese American, Korean American, and Vietnamese American cultures, as well as from other immigrant and dispossessed families from Iraq and Syria, Ethiopia, and Haiti, who sent their children to public schools.

Children from immigrant and dispossessed families always participate in their communities with vibrant and long-standing knowledge practices, cultural practices, and language practices that enable them to solidify membership in their cultural communities, despite having suffered in journeys to this nation. Children are resilient and full of life and the capacity to learn. Teachers who embrace culturally responsive pedagogies can tap into children's resiliency and love for learning when they recognize the contributions these children and their families make to the communities in which they reside.

Lest we forget, U.S. public elementary and secondary schools were developed to assimilate and socialize immigrant children, children of color, children who are read as different, children who are believed to have deficient cultural beliefs and practices, into the ideals of American society, as defined by settlers and colonizers, and ultimately those who are hired to teach them. In a post-settler colonial world, language and cultural diversity and inclusion mean that schools, principals, counselors, and teachers need to be much more aware of and be able to change curricula and teaching practices.

These practices were created to benefit the dominant cultural groups and, at the same time, to deny access to, participation in, and benefit from schooling to minoritized cultural groups, including African Americans,

Mexican Americans, Filipino Americans, and Native Americans, as well as immigrant children and children of displaced families who also contribute to the fabric of U.S. society. The authors in this volume provide readers with a wide range of pedagogical practices and knowledges that have the potential for change, to the extent these practices and knowledges become part of the daily school experiences of all children, and most especially for immigrant and dispossessed children. I end with a simple suggestion: Keep learning and help others.

REFERENCES

Faltis, C. 2012. "Art and Text as Living Inquiry into Anti-Immigration Discourse." *International Journal of Multicultural Education* 14 (2): http://ijme-journal.org/index.php/ijme/issue/view/23.

Faltis, C., and B. Arias. 2007. "Coming Out of the ESL Ghetto: Promising Practices for Latino Immigrant Students and English Learners in Hypersegregated Secondary Schools." *Journal of Border Educational Research* 6 (2): 19–35.

Gifford, B. R., and G. Valdés. 2006. "The Linguistic Solation of Hispanic Students in California's Public Schools: The Challenge of Reintegration." *Yearbook of the National Society for the Study of Education* 105 (2): 125–54.

Ogbu, J. U. 1987. "Variability in Minority School Performance: A Problem in Search of an Explanation." *Anthropology & Education Quarterly* 18 (4): 312–34.

Suárez-Orosco, C., I. Todorova, and J. Louie. 2005. "Making Up for Lost Time: The Experience of Separation and Reunification among Immigrant Families." In *The New Immigration: An Interdisciplinary Reader*, edited by M. Suárez-Orosco, C. Suárez-Orosco, and D. Boalin Qin, 179–96. New York: Routledge.

"WELCOME TO AMERICA"

Sara Abou Rashed

Bring us your oppressed, your exhausted bodies,
your hungry, unheard crowds and we shall set them free

"I'd like to welcome you to the one and only,
the greatest America." Says the lady
in the white shirt behind a desk.
"Now honey, please fill out all these papers,
and don't forget to send us your story,
why you came here, your hopes and expectations.
We wish you a happy life."
. . .
16 springs I've witnessed, not one
was blooming, there,
behind the shores of the Mediterranean,
everything is a martyr, there –
we don't dare live lest we die,
even roses grow stripped of colors.

Though, the scarred walls there memorize
our names, though the tarred roads
there know our stories.

But here,
to every ally, to every town,
I must introduce myself:
No, no, I am sorry, I am not who

you think I am.
No, I am not who they say I am.

See,
I am as much of a human as you are;
I brush my teeth, I sleep, I cry when hurt and bleed when injured,
I walk the land you walk, I breathe
the same air you breathe, your American dream
is my dream, I am afraid of what you're afraid of.

Please, don't stop me on streets to ask what Jihad is,
don't mistake me for one of them, don't stare at me like an alien,
like a one-eyed, four-legged, green monster of your nightmares.

I am a woman of faith,
a citizen not a suspect.
I carry a breaking heart within, I hold mics not guns –
my story refuses to be told in bullets and word limits.

And no, I don't celebrate the death of children,
I don't wish to destroy homes and churches.

Trust me, I know what loss smells like:
the way fear and revolution play tug of war
on doorsteps, uproot loved ones from
framed pictures on walls, steal a father
from the dinner table – I can only hope
mine hears me now.

I know what loss smells like from a mile far, the way friends
tell you they saw your house tear asunder
like it was never there:
the old gate, the dolls, grandma's garden and every
dream we've built on the roof with hands too small
to plant hatred.

Still, some fear me, they call me names, they try to break
me, to wreck me, to ricochet me, but
my spine will keep mountains standing,
my knees will only ever kneel to my Lord:

Lord, make us whole again, all of us, make us human again,

forgive us for we have sinned, and Lord,
guide them to see me for who I am, because
I, too yearn for peace, because I drop poems, not bombs.

(Originally published in *Pudding Magazine: Journal of Applied Poetry*, Fall 2016.)

INTRODUCTION

Immigrant Tales as Old as Time

Ruth McKoy Lowery, Rose M. Pringle, and Mary Ellen Oslick

Immigration in the United States of America is as old as the country's history. Across time and space, everyone can trace the beginning of their family ancestry to another country. Although many family lineages are now embedded in what is regarded as the American heritage, the sifting of who belongs or who is new still continues to paint our great landscape. Furthermore, despite the long history of immigration, oscillation between the perception of immigrants as a valuable resource and as a major challenge has become central in the political and public spheres. Specifically, debates have become heightened around the role of the United States in humanitarian protection at a time of record global displacement and its national security that have become drivers in discussions about economy and global competitiveness.

Information compiled by government institutions continue to highlight the increasingly diverse population of the United States. According to the Census Bureau's 2016 American Community Survey, the U.S. immigrant population is upward of 43 million people. In addition, data provided by Zong, Batalova, and Hallock (2018) reveal immigrants and their U.S.-born children now number approximately 86.4 million people, or 27 percent of the total U.S. population.

As the top destination for immigrants, the diversity among the population has implications for the evolving nature of the social, economic, political, and educational interweaving into the fabric of the United States. A nation built on immigration and with a burgeoning immigrant population has to grapple with constructs such as social justice, acceptance, and the valuing of cultural and historical identities, and an educational structure that is interwoven with and addresses issues such as cultural relevance.

SOCIAL JUSTICE

Immigrant populations and their cultural, linguistic, social, and life experiences are on the margin of America's society. Such marginalization has implications for all facets of their lives as functional citizens signaling a need for social justice. Simply stated, social justice is the process of identifying oppression in all forms and the ability to identify how oppression is perceived and how that perception relates to one's self and the world at large (Heybach 2009).

Social justice is not simply a disposition that should be taught to students that have been marginalized by society. On the contrary, social justice—as it is as fundamental as the Pledge of Allegiance—should be ingrained in the very essence of education for all students in a democratic nation, regardless of their perceived "place" within society. Within the tension of current immigration debates, the nexus between social justice and education illuminates the problematic relationship between society and the existing political affairs. However, providing students with a quality education grounded in a social justice stance toward solving inequalities will require the formation of authentic and equal partnerships that include state, multinational corporations, policy makers, and educators (Zajda 2010).

IDENTITY

Establishing a positive ethnic identity is important for the psychological well-being of students (Birman, Weinstein, Chan, and Beehler 2007). A three-year study by Phinney and Chavira (1992) shows that self-esteem and ethnic identity are significantly related to each other in adolescent minorities. When students develop positive ethnic identities, they also tend to develop higher self-esteem. This is especially important because children of immigrant parents have increased difficulty in maintaining their sense of self-worth. Blanco-Vega, Castro-Olivo, and Merrell (2008) in their study of Latino students, one of the fastest-growing immigrant groups in the United States, determined that students who have high self-esteem and a positive self-concept are more likely to thrive academically than their counterparts who do not have confidence in their skills and abilities.

Self-esteem and ethnic identity are also inextricably linked to the presence of shared-culture role models in students' lives. Karunanayake and Nauta (2004) determined that students do well when they have role models of the same race. Finding others with similar backgrounds gives immigrant students comfort (Baghban 2007). These role models have implications for students' sense of self-worth and long-term goals:

> Young people learn the racial and gendered structuring of the culture in which they live by noting the race and gender of adults in different professional positions. The presence or absence of like others in different social positions implicitly conveys information to young people about the possibilities for their futures. (Zirkel 2002, 357)

Zirkel concluded that students who had at least one race-matched role model performed better academically, had more "achievement-oriented" goals, and took more pleasure from "achievement-relevant" activities than their peers without such a role model.

It is the responsibility of educators to expose immigrant students to appropriate role models and to embrace the cultures and values from the diverse immigrant populations. Enacting such instruction and curricula in schools will give credence to the immigrants' experiences and identities while enhancing their learning opportunities.

OVERVIEW OF THE BOOK

There are nine chapters in this book, excluding the introduction. The chapters are further divided into three sections, highlighting important aspects of immigration and the experiences of immigrants as they aspire to a new life and a new beginning in a land that historically has been a beacon of hope. Section I presents research narratives of different immigrant experiences from a theoretical lens. Section II shares stories of immigrants, teachers who work with immigrant students, and those who prepare teachers to work with immigrant students in their future classrooms. Section III presents a compilation of resources on immigrants that can help as teachers and others work with immigrant students and their families.

Sara Abou Rashed's poem, "Welcome to America," is a fitting opening to a book that seeks to explore the struggles of immigrants who have accepted the welcome into a land of promise. Her poetic flair captures the essence of a welcome she accepts but that is now challenging her geographical and cultural past—a challenge born out of misconceptions and fear. Sara compares and contrasts her experiences over space and time and very creatively establishes that, oppressed and exhausted, she now seeks to be *set free* from her fair share of loss and pain.

Section I comprises chapters 1 through 5, presenting immigrants' stories as counterstories that challenge the master narratives that have evolved in the current hypersensitive and political environment. Each story offers insights into structures within the socio-educational framework that have the potential to allow new possibilities to emerge and more importantly provide pragmatic suggestions for change. In chapter 1, authors Donna Sabis-Burns and Ruth McKoy Lowery present experiences of American Indian/Alaska Native students and the struggle for an equitable education. Chapter 2 by Youmna Deiri confronts the misconceptions of the amalgamations of Arab immigrants and their representation within the context of terrorism. She shares the experiences of two siblings, Ayman and Omar, and the stereotypes and biases within the walls of schools to highlight the plights of Arab immigrant students. Chapter 3 by Ivy Haoyin Hsieh shares the story of the Chen family, who struggled in the restaurant business and whose lives were different from the stereotypical model immigrant experience. In chapter 4, Cody Miller and Kathleen C. Colantonio-Yurko explore the schooling experiences of three high-performing Filipino students with mastery of standard American English. These students, though successful, were on the margin of mainstream culture and to survive accepted the predominant cultures and values of the institution. Finally, in chapter 5, Xiaodi Zhou and Danling Fu advocate six principles of culturally responsive pedagogy applicable to the U.S. classrooms for working with immigrant students.

Section II, "Reflection and Advocacy," encompasses chapters 6 through 8. These stories, though personal and unique, serve as a form of empowerment, offering hope and the realization that each immigrant's experiences are not isolated. Chapter 6 by Ruth McKoy Lowery, Cheryl Logan, and Deandra J. McKoy shares stories of teachers and their work to engage meaningfully in culturally relevant teaching in classrooms with high populations of immigrant children. In chapter 7, Garfield Daley's story provides a vivid expression of his experiences as an immigrant and his struggle to navigate the terrains of both an educational system and subsequent employment in the United States Finally, chapter 8 by Ann M. Dillard, an immigrant herself and a licensed marriage and family therapist, shares her work with immigrant populations and provides professional development support to educators in the areas of mental health and cultural diversity.

Section III consists of chapter 9, a comprehensive resources list. Mary Ellen Oslick, Marla Goins, and Shawn Anderson Brown, in responding to the need for information on immigrants and immigrant populations, compiled a list of resources with brief summaries, applicable and relevant to support teachers' development of requisite knowledge and skills.

Immigrants will, even amid current political constraints, continue to be woven into the fabric of the United States of America. Education will continue to have a pivotal role in assimilation and the maintenance of the incoming cultural, linguistic, social, and life experiences of the immigrants. It is therefore important to keep the issue of immigration at the forefront when deciding on educational policies, principles, and practices.

This book raises the importance of learning from past mistakes, seeking to create a more welcoming space with open dialogue, and encouraging wider participation in deciding the agenda that influences issues of immigration. Violence and the range of differences among humans have been the causes of wars resulting in mass migration as people flee dangerous lands in hopes for a better world for their children.

The United States historically has offered hope for those seeking a new life. However, this notion has waned in recent times. In the age of global citizenship, a nation is richer by the many interwoven fabrics, its diverse citizenry. An effective education for all is important toward developing functional and contributing citizens and maintaining the notion of the United States of America as the beacon of hope.

REFERENCES

Baghban, M. 2007. "Immigration in Childhood: Using Picture Books to Cope." *The Social Studies* 98 (2): 71–76.

Birman, D., T. Weinstein, W. Y. Chan, and S. Beehler. 2007. "Immigrant Youth in U.S. Schools: Opportunities for Prevention." *The Prevention Researcher* 14 (4):14–17.

Blanco-Vega, C. O., S. M. Castro-Olivo, K. W. Merrell. 2008. "Social-Emotional Needs of Latino Immigrant Adolescents: A Sociocultural Model for Development and Implementation of Culturally Specific Interventions." *Journal of Latinos and Education* 7 (1): 43–61.

Heybach, J. 2009. "Rescuing Social Justice in Education: A Critique of the NCATE Controversy." *Philosophical Studies in Education* 40: 234–45.

Karunanayake, D., and M. M. Nauta. 2004. "The Relationship between Race and Students' Identified Career Role Models and Perceived Role Model Influence." *The Career Development Quarterly* 52 (3): 225–34.

Phinney, J. S., and V. Chavira. 1992. "Ethnic Identity and Self-Esteem: An Exploratory Longitudinal Study." *Journal of Adolescence* 15 (3): 271–81.

Zajda, J. 2010. *Globalisation, Ideology and Education Policy Reforms.* Dordrecht: Springer.

Zirkel, S. 2002. "Is There a Place for Me? Role Models and Academic Identity among White Students and Students of Color." *Teachers College Record* 104 (2): 357–76.

Zong, J., J. Batalova, and J. Hallock. 2018. "Frequently Requested Statistics on Immigrants and Immigration in the U.S. *The Online Journal of the Migration Policy Institute.* https://www.migrationpolicy.org/article/frequently-requested-statistics-immigrants-and-immigration-united-states.

Section I

Research Narratives

I

YOUR LAND! MY LAND! OUR LAND!

American Indian/Alaska Native Students in Schools

Donna Sabis-Burns and Ruth McKoy Lowery

"As a group, Native American students are not afforded education opportunities equal to other American students. They routinely face deteriorating school facilities, underpaid teachers, weak curricula, discriminatory treatment, and outdated learning tools . . . debilitating poverty and lack of adequate federal funding." (United States Commission on Civil Rights [USCCR] 2003, 111–12)

It was February in rural Alaska. Donna was asked to visit a few school sites that were receiving federal grant money for educational programs funded by the U.S. Department of Education. This trip was to monitor and check compliance to federal guidelines and to ensure funds were being spent as expected. After flying over the most desolate tundra in a two-seater plane, the only way to get to this village, Donna arrived on a small gravel strip on a narrow piece of land. She was escorted to the boardwalk that outlined the walkways between homes and community, staring at the hanging, dried fish as she passed the small housing units. There were no roads, no sidewalks; boards fitted closely together on top of frozen mud made a trail leading from one area to another by means of a four-wheeler or by foot. The population was 311 people, 90 of whom attended the preK–12 school. The school was clearly the most modern building there; however, the school leaders and administration rotated out like a revolving door. The school was struggling to meet basic proficiency levels for clear reasons—they could not keep teachers or principals at the school. They were not experienced with the culture nor were they experienced with the harsh living conditions, even though their homes prepared for them, like the school, were the only structures in the community with modern plumbing in them. The school was a solid structure with central heating and stood out as a shining star compared to the other structures along the boarded path. It was clear that this community valued education, but these students were not getting fair or equitable opportunities to grow with revolving door administration or inexperienced/unfit teachers. With a heavy heart, Donna listened to parents, staff, community leaders, and students share their concerns and soon said goodbye, as she had to catch her flight before the harsh wind set in.

Next, she flew to another village to see how their preschool program was working. She was led into a building where there was no lighting at first, but as they traveled the hallway, rays of light came not from a window but rather from the moldy and leaking ceiling above them. They had to dodge broken furniture and falling ceiling tiles to get to the preschool classroom. As Donna walked into the room, she passed the bathroom area. To her surprise, there were no toilets, only a yellow bucket in a wooden stall with no door. There was no running water in this village. Honey buckets were used as toilets and dumped outside the school grounds when they needed to be emptied. Donna wondered inwardly, "This is the twenty-first century and this is part of the United States of America. How are the inequities so vast? How do these children learn with their basic school needs not met? How can we provide a better environment conducive to learning with culturally appropriate curriculum for such a culturally rich people?" These visits changed her life and views toward equity in education, especially for the American Indian/Alaska Native students. Equality may be a subjective concept with widespread historical bearings, but culturally relevant teaching (CRT) is not. CRT needs to be incorporated in all facets of the learning experiences for ALL students.

The state of education for Native students in the nation's K–12 schools is distressing, as the opening epigraph from the United States Commission on Civil Rights indicates. Although Native families existed before the recorded settling of the Americas, the plight of many groups centuries later is still steeped in hardship. While not a part of the recent immigrant groups often discussed in popular media and the context of schooling, the problems American Indians face are similar or sometimes more demoralizing than recent immigrant groups. The experiences of American Indian/

Alaska Native (AI/AN) students face in attaining an equitable education is still less than acceptable as indicated by the USCCR's finding in the opening epigraph.

The North American continent is home to over five hundred and fifty distinct Native cultures (Lohse 2008). Riley (2013) determined that when Europeans journeyed to the Americas, they encountered "hundreds of indigenous, sovereign nations representing enormous diversity in terms of language, culture, religion, and governance" (371). In contemporary eras, American Indian/Alaska Native families have faced near impossible hardships as they work to maintain their cultures—some cultures have disappeared, many have survived, and still others struggle to survive. Native people throughout the United States have continuously attempted to regain the practices that helped define them as a people and within their communities.

Education, a pivotal marker for success, continues to be important in helping different cultural groups maintain their place in the history of the United States. Many tribes have created dictionaries of their languages, with elders recording their knowledge and memories. Countless other efforts have been made to connect the past with the present. Educational systems have been vital in many of these efforts, as tribal colleges and public schools have worked to restore and catalog this knowledge. Lohse (2008) determined that the federal government has a unique, legal obligation to Native students and families because the educational success of Native students is linked to state and national economies.

Cladoosby (2015), however, asserted that the federal government's "treatment of tribes throughout various periods of federal-tribal policy has been a strong determinant of the type and quality of education Native students received" (2). It is important to be concerned about the educational well-being of native students as a simple moral imperative to ensuring equal educational opportunities for these students. In this chapter, the authors focus on the educational experiences of American Indian/Alaska Native Students, explicating the need for a more culturally responsive way of addressing and improving their educational experiences.

STATISTICS ON AMERICAN INDIAN/ALASKA NATIVE (AI/AN) STUDENTS

American Indian/Alaska Native students generally perform two to three grade levels below their white peers in reading and mathematics. They are more likely to drop out of school and more likely to be expelled than their white peers (Lohse 2008). Lohse further posited that for every 100 AI/AN kindergartners, only seven will earn a bachelor's degree, compared to thirty-four of every 100 white kindergartners. These data represent a snapshot of the current problems facing AI/AN students and their educational attainment.

One contributing factor to the achievement gap between AI/AN students and their peers is that many AI/AN students are not adequately prepared to learn when they walk through the doors of their school. In addition, the effects of poor economic and geographic conditions in many AI/AN communities add to the challenges facing families and schools. Low-income homes, lack of adequate health care, and other factors create additional challenges that add to the achievement gap.

The 2010 U.S. Census estimated the total American Indian/Alaska Native (AI/AN) population at 2.9 million, or about 0.9 percent of the U.S. population. Indian youth have the highest rate of suicide among all ethnic groups in the United States, and suicide is the second-leading cause of death for Native youth aged fifteen to twenty-four (Apthorp 2016). Apthorp also found that more than 70 percent of grade 12 American Indian students nationwide have not demonstrated proficiency in math or reading. Freed and Samson (2004) determined that there are many factors that contribute to the high dropout rates for Native Alaskan students. In South Dakota, where American Indian students account for 14 percent of the student population, their proficiency rate is less than 30 percent in math and reading in grades 4 and 8 (Apthorp 2016).

Higher percentages of American Indian/Alaska Native tend to receive services through special education programs. The percentage of students served under the Individuals with Disabilities Education Act (IDEA) was highest for AI/AN (16 percent), followed by Black students (15 percent). The school dropout rate in 2013 was highest for AI/AN (13 percent) compared to Asian students who had the lowest rate (2 percent) (Kena et al. 2016).

In the 2013–2014 school year, only 69.6 percent of AI/AN students graduated high school in four years, compared with 82.3 percent of the total U.S. population (National Center for Education Statistics 2015). The AI/AN graduation rate was the lowest among all races/ethnicities, and even lower than economically disadvantaged youth. Lopez (2018) has determined that the number of AI/AN students who pursue postsecondary education is lower than any other ethnic group in the United States.

A BRIEF HISTORY OF AI/AN EDUCATION

The education of AI/AN students has its roots in American history unlike other minority groups in the United States (Brief History 2018). For centuries, AI/AN children have suffered with inequitable policies and procedures that have oppressed a population of people into a "sink or swim" method of survival (McCarty 1993). High dropout rates, low-test scores, and high poverty have been and continue to be areas of concern within this minority group. Several research studies support the need for transition strategies for American Indian students (Freed and Samson 2004; Nolan 2013). A brief summary of the history of Indian education and its correlation to federal Indian policy is presented in appendix A.

Through extensive testimonies from citizens and educators, school site visitors like Donna in the opening epigraph, and commissioned papers from experts, the Indian Nations At Risk Task Force was formed in 1991. The task force developed a systematic study to analyze the current state of Indigenous people in the United States and made recommendations on how to improve the quality of life. Because of this study, the task force presented their findings at a White House conference on Indian education. They identified four findings why Indigenous nations are at risk as a people:

1. failure of schools to educate large numbers of indigenous students;
2. the erosion of native languages and cultures;
3. threats of further reduction of native lands and natural resources; and
4. challenges to indigenous self-determination and governance by changing federal policies and court decisions.

Educators and those concerned with the education of AI/AN students need to be aware of the historical impact on the state of American Indian education today in order to provide sustained help for them. Further, they should work to eradicate the inequities in the educational experiences for these students, seeking a more culturally responsive way to create a more sustainable educational environment, especially in areas that have difficulty hiring and retaining teachers and school administrators.

EDUCATING FOR CHANGE: CULTURALLY RESPONSIVE TEACHING FOR AI/AN STUDENTS

Freed and Samson (2004) have posited that one-third of Alaska's school districts, particularly districts in rural and remote areas, face teacher shortages. This chronic shortage happens as teachers find it difficult to adjust to the living conditions in the villages. Some teachers even leave without spending one day in the classroom. It is important to prepare a cadre of teachers and administrators who are better equipped to meet the needs of these students, teachers who are culturally responsive and who can bring about positive change for many struggling villages and school districts.

Preparing culturally responsive teachers is easier to talk about but less so to realize. It means preparing teachers who understand what the teaching conditions will be like when they go out to teach in an area unlike cities and towns they grew up in. Culturally responsive programs prepare teachers who learn to build communities and form alliances with parents and communities to facilitate a rounded learning experience for all students.

According to Lee and Quijada Cerecer (2010), it is important for teachers to think beyond students' cultures to preparing them to use their cultures to live in the present. Teachers must first understand the lived experiences of their students and then move forward to help them see how they can augment those experiences with the education they receive in schools. Far too often, teachers find themselves in classrooms filled with ethnically and racially diverse students yet they do not know or recognize the value of diversity and the importance of culturally responsive pedagogy. Geneva Gay (2015) determined that teachers' beliefs about ethnic, racial, and cultural diversity determine their instructional behaviors, and cultural bias is born.

Preparing Culturally Responsive Teachers for the Classroom

In advocating for an inclusive and improved pedagogy for teaching, noted scholar Gloria Ladson-Billings (1995) articulated three important criteria for culturally relevant teaching: "a) Students must experience academic success; b) students must develop and/or maintain cultural competence; and c) students must develop a critical consciousness through which they challenge the status quo of the current social order" (160). For this to happen, however, students need teachers who are prepared to help them get to this point, teachers who espouse these values and help students to actualize their potentials.

For many American Indian/Alaska Native students, like the students Donna visited in rural Alaska, their education is hindered by the constant revolving doors of teachers ill-prepared to teach culturally and racially diverse students. It is critically important for this to change. Two areas of immediate change that can help AI/AN students experience more meaningful and culturally relevant education are (a) teaching and preparing non-AI/AN teachers and (b) preparing more AI/AN teachers to integrate and transfer their indigenous knowledge of community and culture to their fellow culturally connected students.

Preparing non-AI/AN teachers to be more "culturally aware" and reflective in their pedagogical practices is essential for AI/AN students' educational success. These teachers must be prepared to move away from mainstream educational practices and conditions to critically contemplate the needs and backgrounds of their AI/AN students. Gay (2013) argued that culturally responsive teaching should center and preserve the culture of the group being educated. Gay further determined that it is important to change the deficit thinking modality of teaching minoritized students to focus on "strengths, promises, and possibilities" (68).

Another important goal in preparing culturally responsive teachers is to actively recruit and train American Indian/Alaska Native teachers. Among the benefits of training AI/AN teachers to teach in their own AI/AN communities is that these teachers bring with them a strong knowledge base and familiarity with the cultural nuances and attributes essential to teaching Native students that do not result from formal training

(Beaulieu 2006). Beaulieu further determined that AI/AN teachers have a better understanding of their communities and of the families of the children who have grown up within the same community.

AI/AN teachers are already culturally aware, thus sensitivity training is not the main focus of preparation. However, it is important to provide training programs that emphasize how to assist AI/AN teachers in rendering their unique experiences and natural cultural training into effective instructional and curricular strategies. This grassroots method of providing teacher preparation programs in the local schools, where teachers can learn while working with students, prevents interrupted learning for the students. It creates stable school personnel, thus preventing the revolving door exodus.

CONCLUSION

Despite a wide array of curricula related to American Indian cultures, existing literature presents information about how to learn about "Indians" rather than how to implement a culturally appropriate curriculum. Educational researchers and practitioners have long advocated adopting a culturally appropriate curriculum to strengthen the education of Native youth (Yazzie 1999). Such an approach uses materials that link traditional or cultural knowledge originating in Native home life and community to the curriculum of the school.

Apthorp (2016) posited that American Indian students succeed academically when their Native culture is integrated into curricular and extracurricular activities in school. For example, research in Alaska and Hawaii indicates that students whose coursework is aligned with state content standards and integrated with Native culture advance in academic achievement statistically significantly more than students whose coursework is not. Preparing Native teachers to teach AI/AN students is one step in creating culturally appropriate curricula.

Preparing teachers to meet the needs of American Indian/Alaska Native students is imperative if these students are to attain an equitable education. The conditions of the different school environments Donna visited in rural Alaska highlight the pressing need for these changes. Preparing non-Native teachers who are committed to live in and among these students, working with parents and the community to meet their needs, is important. More important is the need to prepare Native teachers who already understand the cultural mores of these populations, thus minimizing the persistent turnover of teachers and school administrators. Cladoosby (2015) succinctly posited,

> It is vital that we all work together to strengthen our human capital in all tribal communities across America. The most effective way to do that is to provide a high-quality, culturally-appropriate education that effectively and equally benefits all of our nation's children—including our Native children. (1)

Questions to Guide Teachers' Facilitation of AI/AN Students in the Classroom

1. What steps can I take to avoid using a "tourist" curriculum approach to teach AI/AN students?
2. In what ways can I integrate students' home language and cultural experiences in the classroom?
3. What strategies can I employ to spark my students' learning?
4. What steps do I need to take to implement a culturally relevant curriculum that meets the needs of all students in my classroom?

REFERENCES

Apthorp, H. S. 2016. "Where American Indian Students Go to School: Enrollment in Seven Central Region States (REL 2016–113)." Washington, DC: U.S. Department of Education, Institute of Education Sciences, National Center for Education Evaluation and Regional Assistance, Regional Educational Laboratory Central. Retrieved from http://ies.ed.gov/ncee/edlabs.

Beaulieu, D. 2006. "A Changing Political Context." In *The Power of Native Teachers: Language and Culture in the Classroom*, edited by D. Beaulieu and A. Figueira, 1–7. Tempe, AZ: Arizona State University.

"Brief History of American Indian Education." 2018. Expanding the Circle, University of Minnesota. Retrieved from http://etc.umn.edu/resources/briefhistory.htm.

Cladoosby, B. 2015. *Examining the Challenges Facing Native American Schools*. Testimony Before the House of Representatives Subcommittee on Early Childhood, Elementary, and Secondary Education: National Congress of American Indians. Retrieved from http://www.ncai.org/resources/testimony/examining-the-challenges-facing-native-american-schools.

Freed, C. D., and M. Samson. 2004. "Native Alaskan Dropouts in Western Alaska: Systemic Failure in Native Alaskan Schools." *Journal of American Indian Education* 43 (2): 33–45.

Gay, G. 2013. "Teaching To and Through Cultural Diversity." *Curriculum Inquiry* 43 (1): 48–70. doi:10.1111/curi.12002.

Gay, G. 2015. "The What, Why, and How of Culturally Responsive Teaching: International Mandates, Challenges, and Opportunities." *Multicultural Education Review* 7 (3): 123–39.

Kena, G., W. Hussar, J. McFarland, C. de Brey, L. Musu-Gillette, X. Wang, J. Zhang, A. Rathbun, S. Wilkinson-Flicker, M. Diliberti, A. Barmer, F. Bullock Mann, and E. Dunlop Velez. 2016. *The Condition of Education 2016 (NCES 2016-144)*. U.S. Department of Education, National Center for Education Statistics. Washington, DC. Retrieved from http://nces.ed.gov/pubsearch.

Ladson-Billings, G. 1995. "But That's Just Good Teaching! The Case for Culturally Relevant Pedagogy." *Theory Into Practice* 34 (3): 159–65.

Lee, T., and P. Quijada Cerecer. 2010. "(Re)Claiming Native Youth Knowledge: Engaging in Socio-Culturally Responsive Teaching and Relationships." *Multicultural Perspectives* 12 (4): 199–205.

Lohse, C. D. 2008. *Striving to Achieve: Helping Native American Students Succeed*. National Caucus of Native American State Legislators (NCNASL), National Conference of State Legislators. Retrieved from https://www.ncsl.org/print/statetribe/strivingtoachieve.pdf.

Lopez, J. D. 2018. "Factors Influencing American Indian and Alaska Native Postsecondary Persistence: AI/AN Millennium Falcon Persistence Model." *Research in Higher Education: Journal of the Association for Institutional Research* 59 (6): 792–811.

McCarty, T. A. 1993. "Demographic Diversity and the Size of the Public Sector." *Kyklos* 46 (2): 225–40.

National Center for Education Statistics. 2015. "Table 1. Public High School 4-Year Adjusted Cohort Graduation Rate (ACGR), by Race/Ethnicity and Selected Demographics for the United States, the 50 States, and the District of Columbia: School Year 2013–14." Washington, DC: U.S. Department of Education, Author. Retrieved from https://nces.ed.gov/ccd/tables/ACGR_RE_and_characteristics_2013-14.asp.

Nolan, B. 2013. "Reports from the Field: Addressing Challenges of Culturally Responsive Schooling for Native American Students in Low Density Schools." *Journal of American Indian Education* 52 (2): 45–57.

Reyhner, J. 2006. "American Indian/Alaska Native Education: An Overview." American Indian Education. Retrieved fromhttp://jan.ucc.nau.edu/~jar/AIE/Ind_Ed.html.

Riley, A. B. 2013. "The History of Native American Lands and the Supreme Court." *Journal of Supreme Court History* 38 (3): 369–85.

United States Commission on Civil Rights (USCCR). 2003. *A Quiet Crisis: Federal Funding and Unmet Needs in Indian Country*. Washington, DC: U.S. Commission on Civil Rights. Retrieved from https://www.usccr.gov/pubs/na0703/na0204.pdf.

Yazzie, T. 1999. "Culturally Appropriate Curriculum: A Research-Based Rationale." In *Next Steps: Research and Practice to Advance Indian Education*, edited by K. G. Swisher and J. W. Tippeconnic III, 83–106. Charleston, WV: Clearinghouse on Rural Education and Small Schools. Retrieved fromhttps://eric.ed.gov/?id=ED427906.

2

CULTURALLY RESPONSIVE PEDAGOGY

Perspectives from a Saudi Immigrant Family

Youmna Deiri

"Why is it called 'world history,' when it is only about Europe and the United States?"
–Ayman

In recent years, the political landscape surrounding Arab immigrants in the United States has become increasingly complex. Often, Arab immigrants find themselves hypervisible in conversations about immigration and immigrants. This chapter highlights the importance of learning about the diversity of cultural, religious, and linguistic practices among Arab immigrant students. It gives a brief review of immigration patterns of Arab immigrants to the United States and the importance of using culturally responsive teaching in classrooms.

Learning from Arab immigrants can help teachers better understand and connect with their students; it also provides ways for them to sustain their diverse cultural ways of being and language usage. This chapter includes narratives about the experiences of an Arab immigrant family from Saudi Arabia and their perspectives on ways to enact culturally responsive pedagogies at the school and the classroom level. By learning about Arab immigrant students and how to incorporate their diverse knowledge into the curriculum, schools can better serve Arab families and communities.

LEARNING ABOUT ARAB STUDENTS AND
THEIR DIVERSITY

Educators are often misinformed about the diversity of students from the Middle East and North Africa and are often unaware of the complexities of their ethnicities, languages, religions, and communities. To be culturally responsive to Arab immigrant students, teachers need to explore certain background information about this student population to disrupt some of the salient stereotypes about them. Defining who is considered an Arab is not easy, as the category is often contested. The term "Arab" has fluid linguistic and geographical boundaries, but is often used to refer to a person who is Arabic-speaking (Magnusson 2015) or who comes from a geographical area designated as an Arab country. However, Arabs are not a distinct racial, ethnic, or religious category (Shakir 1997).

Linguistic and Ethnic Diversity

Arabic is not a monolithic linguistic category. While Modern Standard Arabic (MSA) is the official language of Arab countries, this version of Arabic is rarely spoken at home or in daily conversations (Mango 2011). Arabic has a religious value for Muslims because of the Qur'an; however, the language has a diverse literary tradition and belongs to the Semitic family of languages (Brustad 2015). It holds value for Arabs regardless of faith. Arabic is a language with diverse literatures and dialects, and it is used for everyday communicative practices (Bale 2010).

Arabic is not the only language spoken by immigrants from Arab countries. There are many ethnic groups with distinct linguistic identities living within Arab cultures. Therefore, not everyone who comes from Arab-designated countries is Arab or identifies as such. Imazighen, Armenian, Kurd, and Nubian are a few examples of the ethnic diversity in Arab countries and may serve as ethno-linguistic categories (Magnusson 2015). These ethno-linguistic categories are far from neat. An Imazighen student may identity as Arab or Imazighen or both. Thus, while a student may speak Arabic, he or she may identify with another ethnic group, or may identify as Arab in conjunction with another ethnic category and speak languages other than Arabic, or they may not speak Arabic at all.

Arab is not a racial category, but due to racialization in the context of the United States, Arab immigrant students, like Arab Americans, find themselves caught in a difficult position of rigid racial categorizations and the struggle to understand their identities within zones of "whiteness," "persons of color," and Otherness (Shyrock 2008). Generally, Arab immigrants self-identify by their countries of origin, rather than the generalized category of Arab; thus, they are Syrian, Lebanese, Jordanian, Saudi, or Moroccan (Arab American Institute 2014). Some describe themselves as Middle Eastern, or North African, or may use their ethnicity of origin.

Religious Diversity

Contrary to the general narratives that conflate the terms Arab, Middle Eastern, and Muslim (Naber 2012), not all Arabs are Muslims, nor are all Muslims Arabs. In fact, Arab Muslims account for only 20 percent of the world's Muslim population (Suleiman 2000). Additionally, Arabic-speaking immigrants may be Muslims, Christians, Jewish, or belong to other religious affiliations (Kayyali 2006). Furthermore, there is diversity within each religious category. Some Arab countries are more religiously diverse than others, and Arab immigrant and Arab American populations reflect this diversity.

Arab Immigration

In terms of immigration patterns, a misconception is often expressed that Arab-Americans and Arab immigrants are part of what is only a recent wave of immigrants. Bale (2010), contended that roughly 10 percent of the African slaves were Arabic speaking. Patterns of immigration from Arab countries to the United States have changed during different historical periods.

The postcolonial political instability in the Middle East, and educational aspirations, as well as the need for highly educated workers such as engineers, scientists, and doctors in the United States, have been some of the main reasons for immigration. Immigration to the United States from countries like Saudi Arabia has only increased during the last decade, and approximately 69 percent of these immigrants hold a bachelor's degree or higher (Zong and Batalova 2015).

An increase in Saudi students on U.S. campuses occurred through Saudi Arabia's King Abdullah Scholarship Program, which was created in 2005 and extends until 2020. This scholarship system has encouraged many Saudi families to come to the United States together to continue the education of one or more of their members (Taylor and Albasri 2014). Some of these families become immigrants or have an imagined future of immigration, while others decide to return to Saudi Arabia.

Racialization of Arab Immigrants

Negative stereotypes about Arab and Muslim immigrants are common, often referring to them interchangeably. Abu El-Haj (2008) has suggested that anti-Arab racism in U.S. society and schooling is on the rise and that it will continue to grow. Arab immigrant men are often portrayed, in light of broader anxieties about terrorism, as expressing a masculinity that is misogynistic and violent, while Arab women are viewed as passive victims (Naber 2012).

These common misconceptions manifest in educational environments, negatively affecting Arab students. As an example of how these stereotypes make their way into the schooling experiences of some Arab students, it is worth looking at the stories of two siblings, Ayman and Omar, about how they faced racism at school.

> Ayman, a sixteen-year-old from Saudi Arabia, moved to the United States when he was eleven. In the past five years, he has lived in four different locations. He is the eldest of six siblings; the youngest is two years old. While both parents are pursuing their education in the United States, having a large family means that his parents are barely able to make ends meet. Ayman and his fourteen-year-old brother Omar shoulder most of the responsibilities of the household and caring for their younger siblings, and this alleviates some of the stress on their parents, who are both struggling with health issues. Ayman has encountered racism on various levels. At one school, other classmates have called him "terrorist" and "rapist," among other slurs on recurring occasions. Less acutely, after moving to a new school in a predominantly White but more diverse area, he was asked by some classmates if his dad beats his mom, and if "all Saudis beat their wives." Ayman sensed that in some instances classmates will avoid him once they learn he is Arab. Ayman reports that he cannot control how other people see him but finds what is happening sad. Some of Omar's schooling encounters with racism are similar to those of his brother

Ayman. However, Ayman and Omar handle their encounters with racism differently.

At the age of twelve, while at a rural school, Omar suffered from severe depression and anxiety and had to be homeschooled for a year and a half. This was because it seemed to him that the teacher did not like him at all, and he could not understand why a teacher would outright reject him in the classroom from day 1. The family moved to a new school, where he has been on the honor roll. A year ago, he was happy that his new school "didn't care about where he was from." More recently, he said, "I have to push it out there," speaking of who he is and where he comes from, as otherwise his own experience will be overlooked.

While Arab immigrants in the United States are as diverse as the countries they come from, Omar and Ayman's experiences are not peculiar. They are in some ways similar to those of many male Arab and Muslim students of their age studying in America.

CULTURALLY RESPONSIVE PEDAGOGY

Culturally Responsive Pedagogy (CRP) was first introduced as a set of pedagogical practices for White teachers who were working with children of color in their classroom but who had little or no preparation in ways of questioning the White-centered character of the curriculum or of teaching that are responsive to these needs of these children of color and their parents. Villegas and Lucas (2002) determine that to practice CRP, teachers must

(a) [be] socio-culturally conscious, that is, recognize that there are multiple ways of perceiving reality; (b) have affirming views of students from diverse backgrounds, seeing resources for learning in all students rather than viewing differences as problems to be overcome; (c) see themselves as both responsible for and capable of bringing about educational change that will make schools more responsive to all students; (d) know about the lives of students; and (e) use their knowledge about students' lives to design instruction. (21)

Culturally Responsive Pedagogy plays a very important role in the schooling experiences of Arab immigrant students. It works to proactively dispel some of the salient negative narratives about who Arabs are, while opening opportunities to understanding and knowing about them as students. It helps in highlighting the textured lives of Arab immigrants, their languages and dialectical differences, religions, families, and overall lived experiences. Villegas and Lucas (2002) highlight many ways in which CRP can be enacted in the classroom. I have chosen to emphasize three elements of CRP discussed above, specifically, the second, third, and fourth of the five elements determined by Villegas and Lucas.

Many Arab students do not see themselves reflected in the curriculum in their schooling experiences (Al-Hazza and Bucher 2008). Many of the stereotypical images Arab students encounter in schools do not reflect their lived experiences, their cultures, or their values. This reinforces their sense of being different. Hostility to Arab Americans and Arab immigrants often goes unnoticed in schools within the United States. Many immigrant students learn to deny expression to certain aspects of their identity to avoid being marked as different.

Culturally Responsive Pedagogy is designed to counter such tendencies, enabling teachers to combat the assimilative forces and the vilifying narratives that Arab immigrant students face both at school and in media and political discourses. Educators can help these students to engender more affirmative conceptions of themselves, their language, religions, and cultural practices.

SEEING RESOURCES OF LEARNING IN STUDENTS AND THEIR PARENTS

The story below highlights the importance of understanding Arab immigrant students' families. It focuses on practices of hospitality and the responsibilities some Arab students must fulfill at home, while also highlighting parents' views and anxieties about assimilation. It calls into question some pervasive stereotypes about Saudis regarding wealth, gender roles, and education. Additionally, it shows that in the case of this particular Saudi family, the parents and children understand how they are being situated at the children's school and suggests ways for teachers and schools to be more culturally responsive.

The story provides a window into an Arab Saudi immigrant family, capturing moments of their textured lives, along with conversations about their schooling experiences. The purpose of using real stories is to show the importance of establishing long-term and culturally responsive relationships and social engagement with immigrant families. It also foregrounds the many layers of ethnic, religious, and linguistic identities immigrant parents and students juggle at any given time in their daily life. Most, importantly, it aims to dispel many of the negative and stereotyped narratives about Arab Americans or Arab immigrants.

The story begins with my journal entry and is reflective of the relationship I had with this family over the past three years:

I was due for a home visit during Ramadan, a holy month when some Muslim denominations fast from sunrise to sunset, to one of the Saudi families participating in a larger research project. I have known this family for three years, and I followed their children's schooling experiences, attended parent-teacher conferences with them, and witnessed their transitions between various schools. I texted Sarah, the mom, who is a forty-two-year-old undergraduate engineering student.

يمنى : بقدر أجي لعندك اليوم مشان أعمل كم مقابلة معكن في عندي تسليم بحث وضروري أخلص

Youmna [by text message]: Can I come by today? Because I need to ask you some questions. I have a research submission due, and I need to finish it up.

To which Sarah responded, also by text:

سارة : تعالي افطري معانا

Sarah: Come, break fast with us (breaking fast during Ramadan).

I headed their way, parked my car close to their mailbox, and walked up the front porch. When I knocked on the door, Omar, their fourteen-year-old, opened the door, with the sixteen-year-old Ayman standing behind him, along with their four younger sisters, who were all under the age of six. They seemed piled up in the tight entryway of their split-level home. Omar, with a wide teasing smile, made sure to tell me that he was unhappy with my long absence until now. Ayman ran up the stairs announcing that "Abla," Aunti Youmna, is here. He then disappeared into the kitchen to continue cooking. I walked up the half-flight of stairs to the living room, gave Sarah kisses on both cheeks, sharing our common joke about how I can never get right the number of kisses, as this is different in Jeddah in Saudi Arabia where I was born, and Aleppo, Syria, where I grew up and I am from. Sarah's husband, Hamed, a PhD student, and the father of Omar, Ayman, and their sisters, stood up, moving away from his laptop, and reached out as if to give me a hug.

After conversing for an hour in the living room, Hamed, Sarah, and I moved to the adjacent dining room. At the dining table, Sarah started kneading the dough. She gave it to Omar to stuff with meat and cheese before baking. I started the audio recorder and asked questions about how teachers might make classrooms more culturally responsive and sustaining for their children, the importance this might have to them, and what they would like to be done in this regard. While we were conversing, I tried to help with the cooking, but my cooking skills were questioned, as is usual. Ayman and Omar were alternating their attention between the tasks of cooking and cleaning the kitchen according to their mother's instructions and taking care of their younger siblings. Reem, who is almost six, was helping take care of her three younger sisters. During the three years of my home visits, Ayman and Omar never worked on homework while at home during the school year. They always made sure that they finished their homework at school. With both parents having major health issues, being themselves students and constantly working to make ends meet, Ayman and Omar were often the main caregivers for their younger siblings.

While asking questions about her children's schooling experiences, Sarah revealed strong feelings about the importance of affirming students' values and cultural practices in the classroom, particularly with regard to their children's linguistic, ethnic, and religious identities. She said that she had found on multiple occasions that the teachers seemed unprepared to work with immigrant students, especially those from Arab countries. Sarah, whose personality is more driven and vocally assertive than Hamed's, believed that their children are forced to assimilate to "White" models of thought and behavior and that her parenting practices were constantly being questioned or condemned by her children's schools. She said, "Schools should not force students and their parents into a mono-culture and a specific way of life."

Hamed, who is often more talkative and laid-back, believed that teachers and school administrators need to draw on parents' resources to find ways to engage immigrant students in the classroom. He thought that solutions would need to be top-down but critiqued how everything at schools somehow should come in the form of a checklist. On explaining *top-down solutions, he mentioned that without policies and serious efforts from school administration to encourage diversity, teachers would feel reluctant. In seeking to advocate for his children, he found that he could leverage his educational capital to help in creating culturally responsive solutions for his children at school. He helped one of the teachers at Ayman's school recognize that friendships operate differently in U.S. contexts than in Saudi Arabia. Ayman feels more comfortable relating to Latinx peers, because they understand the importance of family and know that belonging to a group and being honest with close friends and family is essential and more important than being independent and competing for one's own success. Hamed offers a positive example of collaboration between him and the school concerning Ayman's lack of classroom engagement. Hamed believes that for his son to be engaged in class, the teacher will need to build a human connection based on his or her caring deeply about Ayman in ways that enable him to feel like a member of the classroom community. Hamed also suggested that his son would not be likely to want to interact with the teacher without building that sort of essential human relationship of care.*

Hamed believes that schools need to draw on the knowledge and experiences of parents for suggestions and advice about what is best for their children's education and for them to have positive experiences in their school communities. He believes that this can help in counteracting the power of the deficit narratives that he finds prominent in American schools.

Sarah and Hamed are financially disadvantaged in the U.S. context or standards. They receive food stamps, and their children receive free lunches; they are considered significantly under the poverty line for their neighborhood. Moving to a school district with better school ratings meant that half of their income goes to paying their rent. However, Hamed and Sarah have learned the value of their educational privilege and use it to their children's benefit. He and Sarah have developed strategies to get the school to see them as a valuable resource for finding solutions that will ensure better educational experiences for their children.

They have learned about and noticed who gets heard more often at their children's schools and who is able to question a teacher's decisions. When a situation has seemed to call for exerting some assertiveness, as in contesting the child services court case the school filed against them, Sarah would be the one to dispute. Whereas, when a situation required multiple visits to the school, some amount of negotiation, and the requisite patience, this fell to Hamed.

Both parents struggled a long time to develop effective strategies for raising concerns about their children's educational experiences and overall well-being and getting their suggestions heard by the school authorities. Hamed and Sarah recognize their educational privilege and lamented the fact that they had to work hard to figure out how to push for the opportunity to be heard.

As we were conversing, Hamed made sure to check on the food every so often so that it would not get burned. Though it was Ramadan, neither of the parents were fasting, because Hamed is diabetic and Sarah has health complications that prevented her from fasting.

From the standpoint of some Islamic jurisprudence schools of thought, because both parents have serious health issues and complications, they are exempt from fasting. From my conversations with them over the years, I have found that they express varying levels of commitment to their faith, seeing it as a spectrum rather than an absolute, which certainly is not unusual. But it was important to both of them that Ayman and Omar experience fasting and understand it as part of their identity as Muslims.

While all this was happening, the four younger siblings were playing in the living room. My conversations with Sarah and Hamed were mostly in Arabic. Taking my recorder to the kitchen, I tried to talk with Ayman. He tends to be reserved and not very vocal. Our conversation morphed into English right away. I asked Ayman if he ever noticed his culture, religion, or language being represented or talked about in the classroom. "No!" he exclaimed. Immediately, he went on to comment on his history course, which he almost flunked until a substitute teacher took over. This was the only class that he struggled with. He questioned, "Why is it called 'world history,' when it is only about Europe and the United States?" Because of the title of the class, he had expected to learn more about the world. "We spend the entire year on American and European histories," he complained, "and gloss over other histories." Shortly after, I talked with Omar and we moved from the kitchen to the dining room again. I was surprised that his first critique was of his social studies classes, too. He talked about his "the American History class." He emphasized "the" when he talked about his American history class, indicating its singularity. But he noted that in the previous year he had said, "I was happy to learn about my own history and culture but was even more happy when I learned about so many other cultures." At this point, Sarah entered the conversation and said, "You know, it is not only about other students. Learning about another culture helps American students." Sarah then wondered if her kids are learning about American history, shouldn't they learn about it from an indigenous perspective first?

Omar and Ayman had critical perspectives on the ways history is taught at the schools they attend. They both showed eagerness to learn about their own culture and language as well as the cultures, languages, histories, and cultural practices of other students in the classroom. Furthermore, Sarah, Omar, and Ayman all understood how these classes are framed in school and how it marginalized them and other immigrant students.

AFFIRMING STUDENTS' DIVERSE BACKGROUNDS AND VALUING DIFFERENCE

The first element of Culturally Responsive Teaching (CRT) is having affirming views of students from diverse backgrounds and valuing their diversity and difference. There are many ways to affirm students' backgrounds, one of which is affirming their linguistic identities, especially when their linguistic identities are marginalized, criminalized, or put to question. Many immigrant students are faced with having to conform to standardized benchmarks of academic achievement that systematically work to diminish the importance of their home languages.

Reem, the six-year-old girl in this Saudi family, speaks Arabic at home. She entered kindergarten when she was five-and-a-half years old. While Sarah and Hamed can both speak English, they have chosen to speak Arabic with their children. Their reasoning is that their children will always be operating in English-speaking spaces. If they do not learn it at home, they will lose their Arabic linguistic identity and, with that, the ability to connect with their own culture and express themselves within it. Given the centrality of family to many Arab immigrants, the Arabic language plays an important role in communicating with various family members who live in the same household, such as grandparents, parents, and children. Sarah related how being in a more linguistically diverse classroom has helped Reem appreciate learning in general.

Reem's teacher learned about the many languages of students in the classroom, identified some examples of bilingual children's literature, and used them in the classroom. She sought parents' help in identifying stories that highlighted important aspects of her student's cultural practices, such as different religious festivities, in books related to Saudi Arabia and to the particular region of Saudi where they are from rather than looking for any bilingual book. To Sarah and Hamed, their children's ability to see their language as well as other languages affirmed in the classroom helped lessen the tensions of the children's struggle between their Arab identity and their being immigrants to the United States. However, there have been many instances in which their children have been penalized and were asked to conform to an exclusive English-speaking culture of uniformity.

BEING AGENTS OF EDUCATIONAL CHANGE

In understanding themselves as change agents, teachers can see themselves as capable of enacting CRT in their own classrooms. Enacting educational change does not have to involve large gestures; it can be showcased in the smallest of actions and be appreciated equally by students from diverse backgrounds. Ayman related that his world history teacher was teaching some "weird thing" about Islam. The teacher was practically saying that "Islam started in Spain. . . . I did not want to engage in this whole situation." He just wished that the teacher would check her sources and learn about other religions from a more informed point of view. Fortuitously, the substitute teacher who came in the next day, after clearly stating that he must teach the lesson plan because they were going to be tested on it, noted that this information about Islam is inaccurate.

The substitute teacher strongly recommended that students read historical accounts from a different perspective than the one provided in the lesson plan. While this teacher did not teach responsively, his act is one that can mediate an environment conducive to Culturally Responsive Teaching. This act was in itself subversive of the overall narrative about Islam that was being taught in class, and Ayman appreciated it. Ayman struggled a lot in this class, which he reported that he tried to pass. He said, "I would have been more engaged if it was real world history." His expectation, based on the title of the class, was to learn multiple historical perspectives and narratives involving places other than Europe and the United States. He recommended that teachers should explain and teach more about the cultures of the students in the classroom and other cultures as well, allocate time for students to ask questions, and dispel stereotypes.

Ayman was intrigued to find that not only Arab students were being stereotyped but also Mexicans and others. As an example to dispelling stereotypes, Ayman said, "We have a Chinese American student in class, and in many instances other students ask him where he is from." Ayman alluded to his desire to learn more about how students are seen differently based on their race. He suggested that teachers need to take the time to talk about these stereotypes and dispel them rather than ignore them. In this way, they can affirm diverse perspectives about students from the same community.

BRINGING STUDENTS' KNOWLEDGES INTO THE CLASSROOM

When asked about a culturally responsive practice that stood out to him, Omar suggested that teachers rely on students' knowledges as a resource. Rather than putting students on the spot by asking them to talk about their culture, Omar fondly remembered how one of his teachers had asked him to help in lesson planning a unit about Islam. Omar said, "There was no pressure to do it," but the teacher consulted him on certain points. One of the suggestions that Omar had for teachers, especially history teachers, is to "go off the book" or curriculum in drawing on the students' knowledge. He said, "I know that we are in America, but students need to learn about out there."

One of the experiences that Omar was most influenced by was when this history teacher incorporated learning about the students' various cultures. When this teacher was teaching about a country, or a religion, he would first, prior and outside of class, run the lesson plan by a student who knew more about the topic and ask for help. Omar was very pleased that this teacher asked him to help in the lesson planning. Being able to have a voice in the lesson planning made Omar feel that the teacher was seeking to learn about him.

The teacher made sure to ask about areas that he was not comfortable with his knowledge, especially related to cultural and/or religious practices specifically related to Saudi Arabia. Simultaneously, Omar affirmatively stressed that it was important that the teacher "did not make it a pressure," saying that teachers need to "respect that students may or may not want to help." By doing so, teachers value student knowledge and bring it into the classroom without pressuring students to speak on the spot or monolithically represent their culture.

CONCLUSION

Using Culturally Responsive Teaching (CRT) requires teachers to become informed about the complexity of the linguistic, religious, and ethnic diversity of immigrants from Arab countries. CRT requires being proactive in creating a classroom environment where stereotypes and biases about Arab immigrant students are dispelled. Teachers must see themselves as change agents at least minimally and take the initiative to challenge negative narratives about Arab immigrants by opening up conversations about them, allowing questions that are framed in culturally sensitive ways, and affirming diverse perspectives about students from the same community.

CRT helps in affirming students' languages, religions, and cultures, and enables them to see themselves, their knowledges, and their families and communities reflected in the curriculum, as their own understanding is welcomed in the classroom. Finally, part of being culturally responsive is dispelling teachers' own stereotypes about family involvement and gender roles for Arab immigrant families. Involving parents in their children's education also may help teachers understand multiple culturally responsive ways of engaging Arab immigrant students in the classroom.

REFLECTIVE QUESTIONS FOR CULTURALLY RESPONSIVE TEACHERS WORKING WITH ARAB IMMIGRANT STUDENTS

The following questions may help teachers reflect on their positions, identities, and biases toward Arab immigrant students. They are intended to initiate conversations that can expand to deeper dialogues in the classroom:

1. What biases, stereotypes, or narratives do I hold about Arab immigrant students and their families and where might they come from? How might they impact and alter my own teaching about and of Arab immigrant students?
2. What stereotypes or narratives do I have about immigrant parental involvement? How might these stereotypes affect how I reach out to parents about their children's schooling and classroom engagement?
3. How can I value and draw on students and parents' knowledge and include it in the classroom?
4. How do my views about Arab immigrants, their families, and communities influence how I include their knowledges in the classroom without appointing them as representatives of entire cultures?
5. How do my views about Arab immigrants affect how I take action when Arab immigrant students face racism in my own classroom?

REFERENCES

Abu El-Haj, T. R. 2008. "Arab Visibility and Invisibility." In *Everyday Anti-Racism: Getting Real about Race in School*, edited by M. Pollock, 174–79. New York: The New Press.

Al-Hazza, T. C., and K. T. Bucher. 2008. *Books about the Middle East: Selecting and Using Them with Children and Adolescents*. Columbus, OH: Linworth.

Arab American Institute. 2014. "American Attitudes toward Arabs and Muslims." Retrieved from https://assets.nationbuilder.com/aai/pages/9785/attachments/original/1431961128/American%2520Attitudes%2520Toward%2520Arabs%2520and%2520Muslims%25202014.pdf?1431961128.

Bale, J. 2010. "Arabic as a Heritage Language in the United States." *International Multilingual Research Journal* 4 (2): 125–51.

Brustad, K. 2015. "The Question of Language." In *The Cambridge Companion to Modern Arab Culture*, edited by D. Reynolds, 19–35. Cambridge: Cambridge University Press.

Kayyali, R. 2006. *The Arab Americans*. Westport, CT: Greenwood Press.

Magnusson, A. 2015. "The Question of Language." In *The Cambridge Companion to Modern Arab Culture*, edited by D. Reynolds, 36–53. Cambridge: Cambridge University Press.

Mango, O. 2011. "Arabic Heritage Language Schools in the United States." *Alliance for the Advancement of Heritage Languages Publications*. http://www.cal.org/heritage/pdfs/briefs/arabic-heritage-language-schools-in-the-us.pdf.

Naber, N. C. 2012. *Arab America: Gender, Cultural Politics, and Activism*. New York: New York University Press.

Shakir, E. 1997. "Bint Arab: Arab and Arab American Women in the United States." Westport, CT: Praeger.

Shyrock, A. 2008. "Moral Analogies of Race." In *Race and Arab America Before and After 9/11: From Invisible Citizens to Visible Subjects*, edited by A. Jamal and N. Naber, 81–113. Syracuse, NY: Syracuse University Press.

Suleiman, M. 2000. "Teaching about Arab Americans: What Social Studies Teachers Should Know." ERIC Document Reproduction Service No. ED442714.

Taylor, C., and W. Albasri. 2014. "The Impact of Saudi Arabia King Abdullah's Scholarship Program in the U.S." *Open Journal of Social Sciences* 2 (10): 109.

Villegas, A. M., and T. Lucas. 2002. "Preparing Culturally Responsive Teachers: Rethinking the Curriculum." *Journal of Teacher Education* 53 (1): 20–32.

Zong, J., and J. Batalova. 2015. "Naturalization Trends in the United States." *Migration Policy Institute, Washington, DC*. https://www.migrationpolicy.org/article/middle-eastern-and-north-african-immigrants-united-states.

3

LITERACY PRACTICES OF CHINESE "RESTAURANT FAMILIES"

Ivy Haoyin Hsieh

No matter the prior experience Chinese immigrants had in their home country, or what jobs they obtained in the United States, it is often believed that the newcomers were professionals, had at least some education in their home country, and had high motivation to learn English (Tung 2000). Chinese immigrants, thus, are mostly seen as a successful, law-abiding, and highly achieving minority group with no difficulties achieving in school (Leong and Tang 2016). The Chen family, participants in this study, have a very different story from the stereotypical image above.

It is important for teachers to adapt a culturally relevant pedagogy in order to ensure students from different cultures have an equal opportunity to learn in school. Teachers not only need to be aware of the cultural differences from diverse students but also need to include students' culture in the classroom (Ladson-Billings 1995). The Chens' story illuminates the importance of being aware of students' home/community environment to avoid neglect and misunderstanding of certain groups of students.

The Chens' story in the United States started with the father, Mr. Chen, the pioneer in the family who was smuggled into the United States in 1992. He arrived in New York City and, like most of his old neighbors, as most newcomers had no connections, lived in very bad living conditions (Fu 2003). Soon after, Mr. Chen discovered the competitive work situation and the bad living conditions in New York's Chinatown; he decided to move out and get a job in a southeastern state.

After he had worked for a few years and saved enough money, he got his wife out of China. She arrived in the States in 1996. Their second son, Tim, was born in 1997 but was sent back to China so that both parents could work in the restaurant. It took them another three years to get their first son, Sam, out of China in 1999. Mrs. Chen won her immigration case in court in 2001 to obtain legal status. They then bought their own restaurant and brought their second son back to the United States. The Chen family was finally settled and reunited after ten years. The ten-year separation had a strong impact on the family members' interactions and resulted in Sam feeling insecure, the parents feeling guilty for not being with Tim during his infancy, and the inauthentic brotherhood between Sam and Tim.

IMMIGRANT LIVES

The Chen family developed new cultural patterns as they lived their lives centered on the restaurant and with limited connections to the "restaurant community" and to the outside world. In order to achieve the American dream, the Chen family understood that they needed to sacrifice the ways they were accustomed to living. The first thing they endured was to be physically separated from the rest of the family.

Even after they finally were geographically reunited, they were still separated in their daily lives because of the family business. Moreover, because their lives centered on the restaurant business, the family did not have much chance or time to interact with the world outside the restaurant. They were isolated in their day-to-day lives, and separated from the mainstream, literate society in their university town.

The Chen children and parents rarely had quality family time together due to their obligations in the restaurant business. The parents worked in the restaurant twelve hours a day, seven days a week. There were no "weekend family outings," no family vacations. Their opportunities for communication and interaction with their children were limited.

According to their work schedule, the family developed a routine that allowed them only a very short time together each day, even though they lived in the same house. The children could not develop a routine since specific routines for eating and sleeping centered on the restaurant's schedule and their parents' working hours. The parents needed to work late every night while the children had to get up early for school. Since it was the only time the children could interact with their parents, they would stay up late and have dinner with their parents at midnight. As a result, the children were late for school often, which led to warnings from the teacher.

Since the parents' primary concern was to work hard to establish the restaurant business, they adjusted their living patterns accordingly. They did not have any long-term plans because they had to make decisions according to the situation of the restaurant. This created a separation from life in the surrounding community. In addition, they were separated from mainstream society by language and cultural differences. Class differences made yet another form of separation in this university town where most of the Chinese/Asian Americans are university employees and students.

The parents and children tried to be as involved in each other's lives as was possible. They also had an understanding that all the sacrifices were to make a better future possible. They did not only live for themselves; they also had to support their families back in their hometown. They held an immigrant ethic that they needed to be successful and they had to honor the family.

The Satellite Chinatown

Being marginalized from mainstream society, the family did not trust the outside world. They believed their house was the safest place in the world. The children locked themselves in the house without interacting with the neighborhood very much. Even though Mr. and Mrs. Chen had picked a middle-class neighborhood, they did not have time to get familiar with the local culture; they were still on the margins, still isolated from the community.

The Chens did not want their children to have a tough life as they had had before, so they tried to protect them in the way that they believed was the best. They chose a university town because Mr. Chen believed life in a small town would be safe, simple, and more comfortable. However, because of the sophisticated nature of a university town, they did not have access to and were isolated from both mainstream American society and the Chinese community.

They kept connected to the Chinese groups in New York City's Chinatown but were not involved very much with local Chinese society. They had relatives in New York City, and they knew how they could get information from them. Because they lived in New York City before they settled in the southern town, their cell phones had New York area codes, they brought food from New York, and they had social celebrations in New York.

Compared with their long-distance interactions with people in New York City's Chinatown, their connections with the outside world in their town were mostly passive. Other than interacting with business partners or customers, they only interacted with a few people who served as mediators in the "university town." Among these people is an active member of a local Chinese church; the other is the principal of a local Chinese school who is also active in the Chinese community. These two individuals represented the high-literate Chinese community. They would engage in conversations with the family when they went to the restaurant and provided help when the family requested it.

The family crosschecked the information they received with their New York community to ensure that it was correct. On one hand, they had to "use" these people as resources to connect with the mainstream community; on the other hand, they still could not stop crosschecking the information they received.

As shown at Figure 3.1, the Chens operated in a restaurant community where they worked together, lived together, and had similar schedules. However, they interacted with people in New York City's Chinatown frequently even though it was physically distant from the restaurant in the university town. The New York Chinatown indirectly connected the restaurant community to their hometown in China. The two-way border arrows show the equal relationships and interactions between the restaurant community, the "Satellite Chinatown," and their hometown in China.

At the other end, the family was connected to the "cultural mediators" they had met through business in town. Through interactions with them, the family could indirectly connect to the mainstream community of the university town. However, the border and the dotted arrows between the restaurant community and the "mediators" show the interactions between them were unequal and sometimes even unnatural. This was different

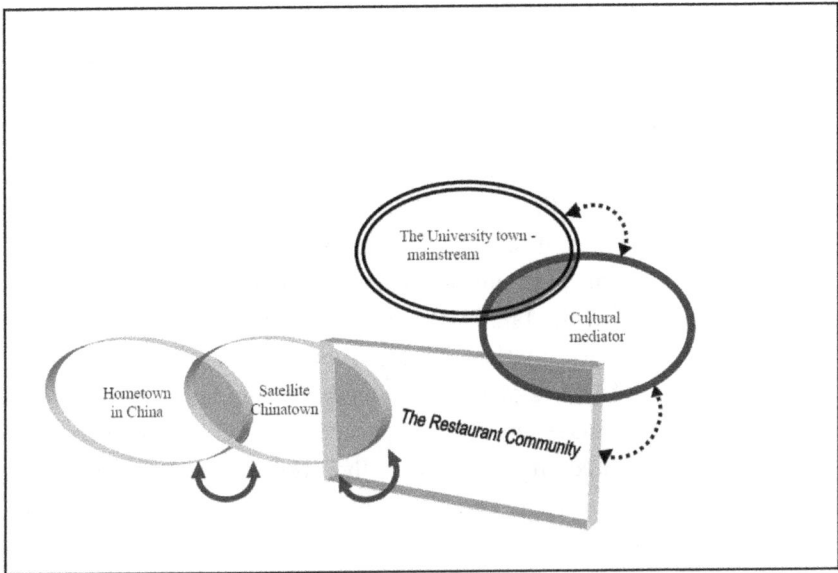

Figure 3.1.   The Socio-Cultural Structure of Family Life History

from the interactions with the Chinatown and hometown communities, which highlights how their social relationships represent a more unequal way of interacting. Through the cultural mediators, the family was seeking a way to climb up to a higher layer of the socioeconomic community.

ROOTED CULTURAL ARCHETYPES

As Cai (1994) explained, "[T]he tradition of Chinese culture values not only loyalty to parents but also encourages brotherhood among friends, colleagues, and neighbors" (175). Confucius's five principles of interpersonal relationships were defined by *Wu-Lun Shu* (a book with detailed descriptions of the five principles) during the Ming Dynasty (1368–1644) to provide different standards for different interpersonal relationships between emperor and officers (or supervisors and employees), parents and children, husbands and wives, siblings (or seniors and juniors), and friends. These five interpersonal relationships are the "central value system" in the social context of Confucian society (King 1985; Yan and Sorenson 2006).

In the Confucian hierarchical system, everyone is supposed to have his or her own role in the family, in the community, and in society. Responsibilities and obligations associated with this role are unspoken but understood and followed by the family. By following this hierarchical system, it was believed that "the whole world is taken care of and is honorable, respected, and at peace" (Heller et al. 2000, 23). This hierarchical system puts family on the top of the list of values in Chinese culture.

Although awareness of society and the nation seem to be the major priority of the system, both entities share the concept of "honoring the family." Thus, each of the family members plays his or her roles following the implicit rules for a father, a brother, or even as a supervisor since traditional Chinese families often work together to run family businesses.

In this hierarchical system, the "emperor and officers" (or supervisor and employees) ranked highest among the five interpersonal relationships. As mentioned earlier, "honoring the family" can be seen as the highest principle in Chinese collective society; thus to be responsible to supervisors and help to make the family business successful is very important and is a way to "honor the family." Under this principle, the relationship that exists between parents and children, known as the Chinese core value of "filial piety," defines the intimacy within families.

Generally Chinese families believe that "blood is thicker than water." They value the family bond and the assigned interpersonal roles in which the parents are responsible for creating and supporting a family, while the children in return need to respect their parents, to obey their parents' wishes, and to take care of their parents when they are old. Having lived most of their lives in Mao's China, the Chen family followed these traditional beliefs and customs in keeping the family values. As a result, while they took the family business seriously as their primary concern, they still created time and space for extended family members to get together.

Hierarchical Structure

As mentioned earlier, for the Chinese, the concepts of a Confucian hierarchical system put people into different layers according to their relationships: with the "supervisor and employees" on top, followed by the interpersonal relationships of parents and children, husbands and wives, seniors and juniors, and, in between, friends. This hierarchal order showed the importance of "family" and influenced how people interacted in a relationship.

Centered by the highest principle of "honoring the family," Confucian values next called for "respecting the parents" (in between parents and children), then "playing different roles" (in between husbands and wives), then "sharing different responsibilities" (seniors and juniors), and finally "being honest and trustful" (to family and friends). Confucian ideas about relationships influence how the family members of the restaurant interacted with each other in their daily life. While most principles are applied in their daily interactions, some may have caused conflicts because of the new living style and the changed family structure in the new land (Yan and Sorenson 2006).

Following Confucian principle, the family placed the restaurant business on top of all other duties and sacrificed their individual needs to conduct the business. Thus, at work, the family members played the roles of colleagues, not relatives. The way everyone interacted with one another in the restaurant was totally business. Traditionally, Chinese people believe that they work not just for themselves but also for the future of the family. They would devote their hard work to guarantee the next generation a better life. In return, they required the next generation to keep up the good work, honor the family, and take care of them when they get old.

Since the most important interpersonal relationship for Chinese is the one between parents and children, the parents expected their children to follow the important Chinese value of filial piety to obey and please them. Therefore, the Chen parents did not want the children to go to the restaurant or to work there; they wanted them to study harder in the United States and get a job that was "better than work in the restaurant." Mrs. Chen kept telling (and yelling at) Sam and Tim, "I work hard for you; you have to study hard in return." She worked so hard to earn more money in order to provide the children a better education. Under this belief, the parents expected the children to be compliant and not to challenge their decisions.

The Chen brothers may not completely understand the deep meaning of their Chinese roles. They felt annoyed listening to the same thing repeatedly. They sometimes got confused about the different roles each had to play in the family. However, although the children complained about the annoying expectations from the parents, they knew how hard their parents worked in order to take care of the family. They still followed cultural rules and took good care of themselves.

Traditionally, the husband is the one who earns a living for the family. On the other hand, a wife handles everything under the family's roof while the husband takes care of everything that is outside of the house. Mr. Chen understood his role and tried hard to play it well. He knew that he was responsible for providing the whole family with a stable life. He had moved to the United States and worked hard to provide his family a better life. As a wife, even though Mrs. Chen had to take on responsibilities outside of the house, she still followed tradition and played her role in the family.

As for the relationships between brothers, in a traditional family the elder brothers or sisters have power over the younger ones. The elder siblings take command when the parents are not home. The younger ones respect and follow the older ones' directions. These unspoken expectations fell on Sam and he complained that his mom expected more of him than of Tim because he was the older one in the family. Even though he had some arguments with his younger brother and was not happy with the expectations, he accepted the role when his parents were not home.

Family Values

Just as Chinese culture highly values family, the family members had their own values and beliefs about the concept of family. Even though the parents tried to be "professional" at work, the relationships were complicated, and it was hard for them to totally divide the two parts of their lives. This was more difficult because of their strong faith in the concept of family. They trusted each other and believed in working together for a good future.

In the restaurant, only the family members got together at the specially designated area to have lunch. The table and the booth that was close to the kitchen had become the "family dining table." Though not written (or even orally) announced, all other workers seemed to understand this unspoken rule and did not cross the line. The other workers knew that the "family" area was a section for "family members only"—even when the other workers needed to help with some jobs close to the kitchen during the non-peak hours, they would not sit at the "family table."

Influenced by Confucian cultural values, most Chinese believe in the power of education. This shows up in the hierarchy of occupations. Among the four basic occupations, scholar is at the top of the social order, then either farmer or businessman, and then laborer. However, not all citizens can afford an education. Even though education is obligatory for all citizens in modern times, many children stay home to help parents in rural areas.

The members of the Chen family came from a rural village where surviving is more important than education. The adult members of the family were not highly educated, because of either economic issues or historical/political reasons. Mr. Chen dropped out of middle school in China. He can read and write in Chinese but not in English. Mr. Chen actually came from a highly educated family, his father being a college graduate. However, after the Cultural Revolution, education was not the only guarantee for a good life. Many parents who suffered in the Cultural Revolution did not encourage children to pursue higher education. According to Mr. Chen, he did not like schooling at all. He started doing business on his own at age eighteen, when China and Taiwan had just begun to have economic relations.

Mrs. Chen did not finish middle school either. She did not read much and seldom wrote in Chinese. After she moved to the United States, she learned to use very limited English to communicate with the cashiers and customers, which she calls "restaurant English." Villagers in the region of China where she is from still follow some traditional beliefs such as arranged marriages, valuing boys much more than girls, and affording boys first chances at education.

Because of the educational background, the Chens were not confident in dealing with people from academic/mainstream society. Chinese parents normally show authority over their children. However, since the Chen parents spoke limited English and they were not familiar with American school culture, they could not check the assignments for the children because they did not have the academic ability. This made them uncomfortable communicating with their sons' teachers.

However, even though they were not very visibly involved in children's school activities, the parents did care about their education. They did hope the children could have a better education in the "dream land." The children did not have the concept of college education. Even the parents did not have much educational expectations toward their children in the beginning. Not until they had more interactions with people from the university town and got more information about college did they start to change their ideas. While the parents thought it was good for their children to work in the restaurant when they just moved to the town, they soon changed their mind to believe that the children should be able to get better jobs than working in the restaurant.

Mr. Chen expressed his attitude to his children's education, "I want them to get as much education as possible, or I did not need to put so much effort to encourage them [to study]." He further noted, "Even if they do not want to, I would force them to [go to school/get education]." He later mentioned that [the children] would be "nobody if you don't get education in this world" and felt regret that he did not have a choice but to work in the restaurant. Similar to Mr. Chen, Mrs. Chen specifically mentioned that she would save every penny that she earned to provide her children the best education they could get. She expressed her hope for the children to study hard and go to the "best university," even if it required her to be thrifty.

Although the adults of the family did not have a chance to have an education in China, they still expected their children to have a better education—specifically a good "American education." The Chens believed that their sons' future can be changed through education and saw this educational opportunity as vital change for and mark of pride for the family.

IMPORTANT POINTS OF INTEREST ABOUT IMMIGRANT FAMILIES

This study provides another perspective of a working-class immigrant family. The Chen family's experiences showed that the literacy culture students bring from families with different cultural/linguistic backgrounds might be different from "school literacy." This experience highlights the importance of teachers' cultural understanding of new immigrant children experiences and their family dynamics and behaviors.

It is important to value knowledge and skills beyond those learned from books and schools and to see the strength of these immigrant families as they work to make their life in American society with limited knowledge of mainstream/school literacy. It is also important to value the immigrant family's experiences and ensure that the children's needs are effectively addressed.

The Strength of the Families

From interactions with the Chen family, it was amazing to see how hard the family members worked to face all the challenges in their life and to adapt to the new cultural experiences and expectations. Even though they were not familiar with school literacy and the mainstream culture and their resources were limited, they grabbed any chance to learn and to connect with the world.

Literacy in Functions

The family members, without fluent English or an ample understanding of American mainstream culture, made their literacies function in different ways and successfully used their cultural literacy to achieve their goal in achieving the American Dream. The ability to run a restaurant, to use the computer, to take a driving test, and to take a flight or a bus to travel with limited understanding of English in an English world should be valued and recognized.

Eliminating the "Model Minority" Label

While Asian Americans often are portrayed as belonging to a "model minority," which reinforces the stereotypical images of Asian Americans as highly achieving and well-behaved (Ngo 2017), families like the Chens may not fit into this category and are thus sometimes neglected by schools and teachers. The superficially positive label "model minority" privileges only certain characteristics of "school literacy" while all forms of literacy should be valued and appreciated. Individuals who work hard and live by positive core beliefs can be models for others.

Toward Cultural Adaptation

All different forms of literacy practices show that families have a strong ability to adapt culturally. The Chens survive in a town where they could hardly communicate or interact well but were highly successful in their restaurant business. They tried to function in a world of English literacy and at the same time retained their own cultural values and beliefs. They developed the ability to adapt to an immigrant culture that enabled them to survive, to be connected, and to be involved in different social worlds.

MEETING THE NEEDS OF IMMIGRANT CHILDREN

Linking Curriculum to Diverse Cultural Backgrounds

Instructional activities that involve tasks related to cultural linkages may create opportunities for immigrant students to solve problems. For example, the boys, Sam and Tim, did not feel connected in school since they seldom had chances to share their cultures in class. Their school life and their family life were not connected and their restaurant background did not help them in engaging their life stories with peers and/or teachers in school. The individual cultures from diverse family backgrounds should be valued and shared in our school curriculum to create positive community relationships.

Connect Students' Social Worlds to School Literacy

Literacy learning relates to the social and ideological worlds, and the relationships and experiences of children and their worlds. Recognizing and appreciating students' out-of-school literacy, encouraging them to bring their social worlds into school, and connecting them with effective resources can improve their literacy learning.

CONCLUSION

According to the U.S. Census Bureau's 2016 report, the number of Chinese immigrants has increased, reaching over 2.3 million or 5 percent of approximately 44 million overall (Zong and Batalova 2017). In the American population, 20 percent speak a language other than English at home; this includes 8.7 percent who speak English less than "very well." The immigrant population is bringing more and more ELL students (English Language Learners) into public school. While some teachers may still believe that ELLs are for English as a Second Language (ESL) education or special education only, the statistics show that every teacher may have ELL students in their classroom at some point. Education programs need to prepare teachers to be able to teach these students from diverse socio-cultural backgrounds.

Among the ELL students, immigrant children who are from working-class families need more attention. Hicks (2002) found that "working-class children" often attend schools geared toward "middle-class values and practices" (3). For these students, it is often hard for them to find themselves in the practices enacted in their daily school experiences. Immigrant children, who are also working-class, indeed need more understanding and care from teachers and schools.

Of course, teachers are busy preparing classes and teaching large groups of students. However, if educators do not try to understand their students' family and cultural backgrounds, they might be missing how to effectively meet their needs. As the population of immigrants and ELL students increases in the United States, the cultures and values from these diverse groups should be included in schools' curricula. It is important to develop deeper understandings in order to create better instruction and curricula.

Confucius's original educational beliefs focused on respect and flexibility. Although his theories and ideas about political rule have long been used by political powers to control the masses, two tenets, respect and flexibility, are still important. Both teachers and students should respect each other as different individuals who can have a positive influence on the other. Confucius stated his beliefs about teaching thousands of years ago: "you jiao wu lei" and "yin cai shi jiao." The first idea, "you jiao wu lei," is from *Confucian Analects* (book 15, chapter 38) where he directly stated that "in teaching there should be no distinction of classes" (Legge 2003). In other words, teachers should treat all students with the same attitude no matter their backgrounds or origins.

The second idea, "yin cai shi jiao," is his core concept of education, which means to adapt different kinds of pedagogies to different kinds of students based on personality, ability, interest, and ways of learning (Tsai 1998). These two ideas are important in creating a culturally relevant and vibrant space for immigrant students like Sam and Tim to feel connected with their peers and teachers.

QUESTIONS GUIDING TEACHER DISCUSSIONS OF IMMIGRANT CHILDREN

1. What can we learn from the experiences of diverse immigrant children and their families?
2. What can we do to accommodate the needs of immigrant students and their families in schools and classrooms?
3. How can we create more inclusive classroom spaces and curricula mindful of immigrant students and their learning?
4. What steps should we take in developing instruction and assessment that meet the learning patterns of immigrant and ELL students?

REFERENCES

Cai, M. 1994. "Images of Chinese and Chinese Americans Mirrored in Picture Books." *Children's Literature in Education* 25 (3): 169–91.

Fu, D. 2003. *An Island of English: Teaching ESL in Chinatown*. Portsmouth, NH: Heinemann.

Heller, C., B. Cunningham, G. Lee, and H. M. Heller. 2000. "Selecting Children's Picture Books with Positive Chinese, Japanese, and Other Asian and Asian-American Fathers and Father Figures." *Multicultural Review* 9 (4): 22–33.

Hicks, D. 2002. *Reading Lives: Working-Class Children and Literacy Learning*. New York: Teachers College Press.

King, A. Y. C. 1985. "The Individual and Group in Confucianism: A Relationship Perspective." In *Individualism and Holism: Studies in Confucian and Taoist Values*, 52, edited by Donald J. Munro, 57–68. Ann Arbor: Center for Chinese Studies, University of Michigan.

Ladson-Billings, G. 1995. "Toward a Theory of Culturally Relevant Pedagogy." *American Educational Research Journal* 32 (3): 465–91.

Legge, J. T. 2003. *The Chinese Classics: Confucian Analects (in Chinese and English)*. Retrieved from http://www.gutenberg.org/dirs/etext03/cnfnl10u.txt.

Leong, F. T. L., and M. Tang. 2016. "Career Barriers for Chinese Immigrants in the United States." *The Career Development Quarterly* 64 (3): 259–71.

Ngo, B. 2017. "Naming Their World in a Culturally Responsive Space." *Journal of Adolescent Research* 32 (1): 37–63.

Tsai, Y. 1998. *The "yin cai shi jiao" from Perspectives of Confucian Analects and "A-han" bible of Buddhism*. Retrieved fromhttp://huafan.hfu.edu.tw/~lbc/BC/3RD/BC0307.HTM.

Tung, M. P. M. 2000. *Chinese Americans and Their Immigrant Parents: Conflict, Identity, and Values*. New York: Haworth Clinical Practice Press.

Yan, J., and R. Sorenson. 2006. "The Effect of Confucian Values on Succession in Family Business." *Family Business Review* 19 (3): 235–50.

Zong, J., and J. Batalova. 2017. "Chinese Immigrants in the United States." Migration Policy Institute. Retrieved from https://www.migrationpolicy.org/article/chinese-immigrants-united-states.

4

COVERING AND CULTURALLY RESPONSIVE TEACHING

Pedagogical Implications from a Student-Led Club

Cody Miller and Kathleen C. Colantonio-Yurko

The purpose of this chapter is to understand how three Filipino American students with high academic standing experienced schooling. Specifically, in this chapter the authors address how the students' cultural identities painted their time in the classroom. Participants' home culture became something that had been reportedly ignored in order for them to succeed in school. This chapter uses Yoshino's (2007) theory of "covering" as a way to understand student participants' reported schooling histories.

Additionally, the chapter addresses how two white teachers (the authors) used Culturally Responsive Teaching (CRT) to create relevant learning spaces in their English-language arts (ELA) courses for students, which resulted in the student participants creating a club that addressed marginalization at school. Students used the club as a way to consider their own positioning in school and advocated that the authors share their stories to challenge the perpetuation of oppressive teaching in other learning spaces. Finally, the authors offer suggestions for how CRT can help teachers support students in their classroom contexts.

STUDENTS AND COVERING

The unique linguistic acumen and epistemologies that students from out-side the dominant culture bring to the classroom come under attack when schools see enculturation into the mainstream culture as their mission (Delpit and Dowdy 2008; Ladson-Billings 2004). Thus, for some students outside of their dominant school culture to succeed they must "cover" their cultural identity. Yoshino (2007), drawing on the work of sociolo-gist Erving Goffman, defines covering as the act of toning "down a disfa-vored identity to fit into the mainstream" (iv). Covering is significantly different from "passing," which entails the minoritized individual being able to be viewed as from the dominant culture. To illustrate, Yoshino uses the actor Krishna Bhanji, who changed his name to Ben Kingsley in order to downplay his Indian heritage. Covering is used to avoid drawing attention to one's "disfavored identity." However, passing is used to pre-tend one is part of the mainstream culture.

In Yoshino's example, Ben Kingsley may "cover" his Indian heritage by changing his name, but he cannot "pass" as a white man due to his skin color. Yoshino argues that Americans' civil rights are in jeopardy because the judicial branch has recently taken an assimilationist under-standing of civil rights laws, which "protects *being* a member of a group, but not *doing* things associated with the group" (173). In short, minori-tized people do not have to "pass" to be protected, but they do have to "cover." Courts no longer protect behaviors; they protect "immutable" aspects of an identity.

The concept of "covering" is a useful tool for understanding the colo-nialist nature of schools and curriculum as Yoshino illustrates; covering forces minoritized people to "assimilate with 'historically white norms'" (23). Students are not forced to pass as white. Indeed, in this study, student participants noted that in order to succeed in school they did have to cover aspects of their Filipino identity, including aspects of their home language and culture.

Yoshino presents four "axes" of covering (2007, 79): *appearance*, which consists of how an individual physically presents him- or herself to the world through attire, grooming, and other surface-level choices; *affili-ation* or how an individual selects to identify with particular cultural identifications such as food, language, and religion; *activism*, which is how an individual addresses political topics related to their identity such as a gay man arguing for same-sex marriage; and *association* or who an individual selects to be associated with whether platonically or romantically. All four axes are crucial to understanding the colonial nature of schooling that forces students to cover along different axes in various contexts.

As Yoshino notes, covering is "a strategy of assimilation available to all groups" (79). It is important to note that these axes can, and often do, intersect. For instance, in this study, a participant may feel the need to cover their bilingualism (*affiliation*) only when around another bilingual student (*association*) in order to avoid being accused of gossiping about a monolingual peer. Therefore, the authors use Yoshino's four axes as avenues to analyze how this specific group of students "cover" in school.

CULTURALLY RESPONSIVE TEACHING

The two researchers in this study used CRT as cornerstones of their approach to teaching their students. As Gay (2010) notes, CRT is a "means for unleashing the higher learning potentials of ethnically diverse students by simultaneously cultivating their academic and psychosocial abilities" (21). CRT aims to empower students and provide them with "academic competence, personal confidence, courage, and the will to act" (32). Furthermore, CRT positions teachers and students as potential change-makers within a democracy.

There is an explicit political disposition in CRT that requires teachers and students to name and challenge injustices inside and outside of schools. Therefore, this approach became important to understand alongside Yoshino's (2007) theory of covering. Researchers drew upon their understandings of CRT to define how responsive classroom practices connect to covering.

While pivotal within the classroom, Gay (2010) notes that teaching alone cannot remedy the inequities within society. In fact, classrooms often reflect the broader inequities and injustices within the society schools are a part of. Thus, culturally responsive teachers need to be aware of the "societal, educational, and ideological contexts" that can lead to some students not receiving the education they deserve (Nieto 2013, 17). CRT requires teachers to be critical and active change agents for their students.

Teachers must work to create more equitable outcomes both inside and outside of the classroom. As teacher researchers studying their former students, the two researchers in this chapter drew heavily on "the four foundational pillars of practice—teacher attitudes and expectations, cultural communication in the classroom, culturally diverse content in the curriculum, and culturally congruent instructional strategies" (Gay 2010, 46).

According to Garcia et al. (2010), teacher education programs need to focus on teacher understandings of diverse students that address "[i]ssues of socialization in and out of schools, and a clear examination of how such understanding is actually transformed into pedagogy and curriculum that result in high academic performance for all students" (139). With such an understanding, teachers could ensure that their curriculum and teaching choices apply the pillars of CRT in appropriate and meaningful ways. As advocated by this study, CRT should be used as a way for teachers to co-construct meaningful and responsive learning environments for students that challenge "traditional assumptions of cultural universality and/or neutrality in teaching and learning" (Gay 2010, 46).

METHOD

The researchers were the participants' previous teachers and, as a result of their close relationship with the participants, students asked them to sponsor a school-based club devoted to "exploring their Filipino identity." The club was founded and led by Luzviminda (all participants' names are pseudonyms). It was through this club that the teacher researchers were able to hear and analyze participants' reported schooling experiences. Therefore, the impetus for this qualitative teacher research study was the participants' continued interest in sharing and discussing their schooling experiences with the researchers. The following section provides information about the setting, participants, and data collection of this study.

Positionality

Before continuing, it is paramount for the researchers to address their positionality. Knowledge and school experiences are "dependent upon a complex web of cultural values, beliefs, experiences, and social positions" (Sensoy and DiAngelo 2012, 8) people inhabit. Both authors are white and taught in a school where the teaching force was predominantly white. The students in this study approached the researchers about starting the club because their positions at the school gave them the institutional power to establish a club and provide a physical space for students.

It was important to ensure that students set the agenda for the club. Both researchers have worked (and continue to work) to understand how their racial identities as white people have provided them with privileges and impact their teaching practices. The researchers recognize that they have been socialized in a white supremacist society and that unlearning racist teaching and research practices is an ongoing process.

Setting

This study was conducted at a small K–12 public school, Palm School (pseudonym), which was affiliated with a large southern university in the southeastern United States. As a result of the school's relationship with the local university, Palm School (PS) had a culture of research and students were accustomed to participating in teacher and university studies. The school enrolled approximately 473 high school students that were nearly evenly split between male and female students.

The school's demographic information was required to resemble that of the state, and so the school's population was more racially and economically diverse than other local high schools in the area because students came from all around the community. The school was 48 percent White, 21 percent African American/Black, 4 percent Asian, and 16 percent Hispanic, and 8 percent of students identified as multiracial.

Participants

The three high school students were eager to participate in the study because they reported that "it was important" for other white teachers and researchers to learn about their schooling experiences. All of the participants were in the eleventh grade and had been taught by the researchers ninth- and tenth-grade EnglishLanguage Arts. The following is a brief description of each participant.

Renaldo. Renaldo was new to Palm High School in the second semester of his ninth-grade year. The son of a stay-at-home mother and retired naval officer, Renaldo was born in the United States and spent his childhood in a Midwestern state. He moved to the South in high school.

Mila. Mila came to the United States when she was approximately five years old. When she was in elementary school, Mila's mother moved the family to her current city. She is bilingual and spoke Tagalog; however, her mother speaks another dialect that Mila somewhat understands but cannot speak.

Luzviminda. Luzviminda held one of the highest GPA rankings in her grade. Born in the Philippines, she was bilingual and had emerged as an advocate of Filipino culture in the school setting. Both of her parents worked in the medical field, and she has a younger sister.

Data Collection and Analysis

As teacher researchers, the authors relied heavily on students' reported experiences and artifacts as data sources (Shagoury and Power 2012). As such, this study sought to understand the participants' perspectives throughout the data collection. In this case study, data were collected throughout a six-month period at bi-weekly lunch meetings. Interviews were conducted during school lunch and focused on students' schooling experiences.

The teacher researchers drew from multiple data sources to strengthen their understandings of the participants' perspectives and to understand participants' schooling experiences (Bazeley 2013; Creswell 2012). Data sources included (1) semi-structured interviews with participants (one-two); (2) one taped discussion (when students shared their experiences); (3) a student-created scrapbook about their experiences; and (4) field notes (researcher and student-created).

Applying Yoshino's (2007) notion of "covering" to the data the researchers gathered from participants illuminates how school policies and practices can ignore the home cultures of Filipino American students in classrooms. Using these ideas, researchers noted that the predominant themes that emerged from the data included "early schooling experiences" and "specific events" (specific memories that the students reported were important to their schooling). Within these themes, students reported instances of when they had to cover in order to accept the predominant culture and values pushed upon them by the institution.

FINDINGS

The following section focuses on participants' schooling experiences and addresses how elementary years shaped their understandings of their identities in schools. Scholar E. J. R. David (2013) argues that Filipino Americans can suffer from a "colonial mentality" in which they internalize oppressive, Eurocentric beliefs about their own cultural identities and practices. The experiences of Luzviminda, Mila, and Renaldo illustrate how schools perpetuate Eurocentrism as aspirational beginning in elementary school. Students like the ones in this study turn to covering as a means of survival in a system meant to force assimilation. The experiences shared by Luzviminda, Mila, and Renaldo offer insight into pedagogical practices grounded in CRT that teachers can use to create spaces where students do not need to cover in order to succeed.

"Don't Use That Word in Here!":
ESL in American Classrooms

Luzviminda's family moved to the United States when she was in elementary school, so she and her sister could "afford the best education in the world." Her mother was recruited by a prominent, local hospital as a nurse, which was common among the Filipino American students at Palm High School. However, Luzviminda did not begin attending Palm High School until she started middle school, in the sixth grade. She was enrolled in a local elementary school when her family first arrived in the United States. Her experiences in the elementary school sent a clear message to Luzviminda about her identity as a bilingual Filipino American student, and that message was to cover the most crucial parts of her identity in order to be accepted.

Prior to coming to the United States, Luzviminda had taken multiple years of English in the Philippines, a process she explains as "popular among Filipino people because they want their kids to have the language of power, English." This trend in her home country was troubling to Luzviminda because she saw it is a form of colonialism: "Some parents don't even teach their kids Tagalog because they're worried they'll have an accent." Luzviminda expressed grave concern that bilingualism was being eroded in her home country. However, she noted this trend was not unique to the Philippines. Her inability to take pride in her bilingualism was made apparent in her English for Speakers of Other Languages (ESOL) course in elementary school.

Luzviminda noted that most students at her elementary school would ask her if she was Chinese or Japanese while others mocked the shape of her eyes. Even fellow Filipino classmates didn't "trust" her because she "looked Chinese." She elaborated that most Filipino American students didn't view her as a fellow Filipino because her skin was "not dark enough." Eventually the Filipino students at her elementary school would accept her, and some would even transfer with her to Palm High School.

Together, she and the Filipino students bonded in their ESOL course, which proved to value English over the "Other Languages." "One time in class I wanted to show the ESOL teacher I respected her so I said *Mano*, which is a way to show respect to elders in Tagalog, but the teacher didn't take it that way. She just yelled, 'Don't say that word!'" She was trying to use her home language to show the teacher respect, but dominant values thwarted her efforts. Exchanges in Tagalog were nonexistent after that incident. Luzviminda came to view ESOL as "English enforcement. It [ESOL education] doesn't honor bilingualism. It wants kids to speak perfect English. It doesn't care about my home language." The class-room, it appeared, was not going to be a welcome place for Luzviminda to bring in her home culture. The rules of school were set and inflexible.

Forcing individuals to cover their bilingualism has a lengthy history in federal jurisprudence. Yoshino (2007) notes that federal courts have long refused to see language as a part of ethnic identity because language is viewed as a choice, thus the judicial branch concluded that if one has the ability to assimilate, one has the requirement to do so. In Luzviminda's instance, her teacher believed she could speak English and therefore she must. Yoshino argues that English-only policies "punish individuals not for knowing too little, but for knowing too much" (138), and English is used as a "marker of intelligence" in colonial institutions like American public schools (David 2013, 80). This was apparent in Luzviminda's case and her excessive knowledge, her ability to speak Tagalog, had to be covered.

After the incident, it became apparent to Luzviminda that she would have to adapt to the standards of American schooling to succeed; standards that were crafted by and for middle-class white students. "I began speaking English only at school and Tagalog only at home. English became my school language. Tagalog is my home language." Although her parents speak English fluently, Luzviminda communicated with her family in her mother tongue as a way to show respect and honor her identity as a bilingual American.

The ESOL teacher may have only wanted Luzviminda to speak the language of power within the school system, but her approach sent a clear message to a young Luzviminda about her home culture and language. Luzviminda's elementary school years in the United States left her feeling as though her identity as a bilingual Filipino American was incompatible with the governing school structures.

"My Parents Wanted Me to Sound Like a White Person": Renaldo's Elementary Experience

Renaldo had a different experience from Luzviminda and Mila because he was born in the United States and identified as monolingual. Prior to coming to Palm High School, Renaldo noted that he was the only Filipino in his elementary and middle school classes. He reported that some Filipino students attended his elementary and middle schools, but they did not interact.

Renaldo considered himself monolingual because his understanding of Tagalog was limited. His parents did not teach him Tagalog growing up because they did not want Renaldo to be viewed as an immigrant: "They didn't teach me Tagalog so I wouldn't inherit a strong accent. They thought this would be better for me in school and later having a job." The concern that Filipino children would need English in order to be successful echoed comments Luzviminda made regarding her own experiences learning English in the Philippines.

The "colonial mentality" makes allegedly "perfect" English aspirational because it bestows the colonized with the tool of the colonizer (David 2013). Renaldo viewed his mother as "too busy" to teach him about his culture. By the time his father retired, when Renaldo was in fifth grade, he took an active interest in "teaching" Renaldo about his Filipino heritage. However, Renaldo noted that he believed it was "too late." Renaldo felt that he was "too old" to "learn" the language. He stated, "By then I didn't know anything about the culture. He tried talking to us in Tagalog, which my mom did, too; it just didn't work out. It didn't really happen."

Renaldo reported that his racial identity became a point of mockery for his peers. For Renaldo, a moment in his fifth grade class stood out: "Some kid told the whole class that I got a 98 on a state test." He further reported that his peers said he received this score "[b]ecause he is Asian" and that "everyone in the class nodded in agreement." When asked, he stated that the teacher ignored the comment. In this instance, the teacher applied the broad stereotype of the "model minority" onto Renaldo.

The fact that Renaldo believed his teachers and peers didn't view the comments as a form of prejudice is not surprising; Lee (2015) has noted the pervasiveness of the "model minority" stereotype as a form of praise in educational settings. During this exchange, Renaldo was being forced to cover his Filipino heritage. Renaldo was acknowledged as Asian by his peers and teacher, but he was forced to cover his Filipino identity and instead succumb to the class's dominant thinking that Asian Americans are monolithic. Renaldo's elementary experience taught him that racial identity would only extend to the broad category of "Asian" in school settings.

"I Relate to Them Even Though I Spoke Little English": Mila's Elementary Experiences

Like the other participants, Mila had both positive and negative elementary experiences. Despite her cultural and linguistic differences from her peers, she still found ways to "relate" to her peers "even though" she "spoke little English." Mila was shy, however, very kind and welcoming, and these qualities drew other children to her. She reported few negative interactions with peers in her younger years. However, in upper elementary she reported a few negative experiences. Mila's pronunciation of words became a point of mockery with some of her peers, and she was very self-conscious. She reported, "My accent was not as fluent." Students also singled Mila out for her food: "Why do you always bring rice? What is the dish you're eating? Sometimes they were more interested than negative about it."

Mila experienced what the Jubilee Project, a project created by NBC Asian America, calls the "lunchbox moment" (Voices 2016). The "lunchbox moment" is the first time an Asian American student is mocked for their family's food at school, which marks them as culturally different from their peers. While she does not recall that these food-based moments were terribly negative, she did feel like she had to take on the role of a cultural teacher and "teach" her peers about her lunch items, which highlighted her "difference" from "other students." However, as she continued her elementary years, she would learn that the tactic of covering would be a necessity to succeed.

Mila's negative schooling memories took place in her English comprehension reading class, she reported: "It was hard for me to understand it." During third or fourth grade, she was introduced to the state assessment, Reading and Writing Assessment (RWA). The school's focus on her success on this assessment was anxiety inducing because she had difficulty with the language and the concept of the test itself. She reported, "Mom was worried I wouldn't understand it fast enough for test." Her mother contacted a private tutoring center and enrolled Mila and her sister in state assessment classes. Eventually, she passed the test.

Coping and Covering in Middle School

Middle school meant transferring to Palm High School for both Luzviminda and Mila. The feeling of not being accepted as bilingual Filipino American students continued to plague Luzviminda and Mila throughout their middle school years. For Luzviminda this meant finding a way to "cope with who she was." Listening to rap music, specifically Eminem, became a coping method for Luzviminda. She referred to the period she "wore hoodies and Eminem shirts from Hot Topic" as a "dark time." However, she found solace and motivation in the music of Eminem. The rap artist's music talked about struggle, acceptance, and being different.

Mila learned to cope with middle school in a different way; she learned to join her own bullies and become a perpetrator of jokes against her race as a way to "cover" her cultural identity. She reported that in middle school "Asian jokes were very bad," because "in elementary school there were [sic] no joking around about race, but in middle school it was bad." Mila came to Palm High School two weeks after the school year had started. She reported that she only knew Luzviminda; however, they were not close. She said, "I would always hear people making racist jokes. It was kinda offensive, but I didn't say anything because I was shy."

Constantly mistaken as Chinese, she remembers one specific group of boys who made fun of everyone in her friendship group. She remembers one of the Asian boys in the group "was made fun of" in the hallways and students would taunt him by saying, "Of course you're good at math!" or "The boy has mad squinty eyes." She recalled that the majority of the people present laughed along.

At first she did not react; however, by the time she entered high school, she had learned to "laugh along with them." Laughing "along with them" became a form of covering in the same vein of Renaldo's silence in his elementary years. Both participants understood that disrupting the monolithic Asian American narrative would marginalize them within their school's social system; they could be "Asian" so long as they acted within the confines of the dominant culture's understanding of "Asian," but they could not be Filipino.

IMPLICATIONS FOR CRT: TEACHERS AND SCHOOLS

As noted above, covering, as examined in this study, is when students quieted aspects of their cultural and linguistic identity so that they could be accepted in the social and academic circles of the schools they attended. The researchers' responsive practices allowed for the students to approach them and advocate for these practices across the country. Students wanted teachers to know about their experiences and provide more responsive instruction in schools to prevent the perpetuation of covering. The researchers suggest that the following key ideas from CRT can create educational spaces where students are not forced to cover.

Teachers must first critically examine their own biases and cultural identities. All people have a racial and cultural identity. However, white teachers must learn how their racial identity has shaped their personal, political, and pedagogical beliefs. If white teachers do not first critically examine their own white racial identity, then attempts to be culturally responsive risk falling short because conversations about race, power, and privilege disrupt notions of "niceness" and "politeness" that are hallmarks of white cultural norms (Bissonnette 2016). Discussing race and culture is often disruptive for white teachers. In that disruption, white teachers can began to unlearn racist socialization. However, being stuck in the discomfort of disruption thwarts white teachers' efforts to be culturally responsive.

Suggestions for teachers are rooted in Sleeter's (2012) guidelines to ensure that teachers employ culturally responsive practices in ways that do not further marginalize students. Teachers should avoid what Sleeter calls "simplifications" of culturally relevant pedagogy. The teacher researchers in this study (the authors) focus on two of Sleeter's "simplifications" that would have created learning environments in which participants did not have to cover: trivialization and essentializing culture.

Sleeter defines trivialization as the process of "reducing" culturally relevant pedagogy "to steps to follow rather than understanding it as a paradigm for teaching and learning" (569). In this study, the school attempted to create an inclusive school environment and did include parents and the community in many school discussions and decisions. While many teachers used aspects of CRT in their practice, there was no formal CRT school plan. As noted earlier, the school's teaching faculty was predominantly white, and the administrative team was completely white. Both white teachers and white administrators were not required (nor provided the space) to critically reflect on their own cultural identities and biases.

Luzviminda noted that her parents never felt welcome at the high school out of fear they would be judged for their "Filipino accents," which resulted in her family being covered from the school. A real commitment to CRT through year-long professional learning opportunities could have provided space for teachers and administrators to critically examine school structures and pedagogical choices that forced the participants to cover. Instead, isolated pockets of CRT could not make up for the systemic oppression often perpetuated in schools.

Sleeter defines essentializing culture as "[a]ssuming a fairly fixed and homogeneous conception of the culture of an ethnic or racial group, assuming culture to be a fixed characteristic of individuals who belong to a group, and that students who are group members identify with that conception" (570). As the participants in this study noted, their peers, and possibly the school, viewed them from a "homogeneous" perspective without deeply exploring who they were.

Luzviminda, Mila, and Renaldo were seen as Asian but rarely Filipino within their schooling experiences. Cultures can also be essentialized through curricular choices. For instance, all three students reported that "Asia" and "Asian American" were synonymous with "East Asian" and "East Asian American" in their middle school curriculum. The institutional power teachers held over students left Luzviminda, Mila, and Renaldo covering their knowledge of the Philippines when teachers conflated "Asia" with the Sinosphere. Providing students with the space to bring in their own cultural knowledge and co-create the curriculum with teachers would have disrupted the essentialized view of Asian and Asian American and prevented students from covering.

Additionally, to ensure that Sleeter's (2012) simplifications are avoided, teachers need to be able to engage in discussions that "provide students with the opportunity to examine and confront the various forms of power, privilege, and marginalization that mark the classroom" (Bissonnette 2016, 12). Those without power and privilege turn to covering in order to avoid further marginalization. The researchers in this study were able to have conversations with the students in the club about systemic oppression and their roles as white teachers in disrupting that oppression. These conversations compose the narratives outlined earlier in the chapter. If more educators in the students' past experiences had been willing to have critical discussions of power, privilege, and marginalization then perhaps the students would not have felt the need to cover.

CONCLUSION

The participants' success within public schools was somehow interpreted as unquestioned assimilation because the students were forced to cover. Their success, traditionally defined through grades and behavior, allowed the school system to ignore the oppressive forces that underpin it and forced students to cover. This has implications for educators. Lee (2015) found that non-Asian teachers and students frequently applied the model minority concept to all Asian American students, which negatively impacted Asian American students.

Our participants had similar experiences. Their previous educators were transferring the stereotype that Asian American students naturally achieve academic success in schools onto their Filipino students, which allowed them to neglect the home cultures of the students. Because their grades were at the top of their class and because they exhibited no "behavior issues," their cultural identity as Filipino American students went unnoticed. In other words, because the participants covered their Filipino identities, they were able to achieve academic success while the school system perpetuated a colonialist assimilation model for Filipino American students.

CRT offers insights into how pedagogy and curriculum rooted in honoring rather than attacking students' cultural identities and practices could look like. As noted by Bissonnette (2016), culturally responsive practices call for teachers to "meaningfully acknowledge" students' cultural backgrounds and this "can radically transform their educative experiences and disrupt the inequitable, hegemonic conditions in which many of them learn" (12). Teachers can honor the cultural identity and knowledge that students bring to the classroom by co-constructing the curriculum to abolish dominant Eurocentric practices and by doing so, allow students to include their own voices and practices in the classroom thus working toward mitigating the need to cover in order to be successful.

Students' home cultures should not be seen as an obstacle needing to be covered for academic success. Rather, honoring, valuing, and incorporating students' home cultures into the classroom should be a goal because it speaks to the truly democratic potential schools unequivocally have but so often fall short of achieving.

QUESTIONS FOR CULTURALLY RESPONSIVE CLASSROOM TEACHERS

1. How can I create a welcoming space for students to share comfortably about their home cultures?
2. How can I work with school administrators and parents to prevent the perpetuation of covering so students do not have to hide their cultural heritage?
3. How do I integrate students' cultural identities and practices in the curriculum?
4. How can I work with school administrators, parents, and community leaders to ensure a safe and welcoming community for our students?

REFERENCES

Bazeley, P. 2013. *Qualitative Data Analysis: Practical Strategies*. Thousand Oaks, CA: Sage.
Bissonnette, J. D. 2016. "The Trouble with Niceness: How a Preference for Pleasantry Sabotages Culturally Responsive Teacher Preparation." *Journal of Language and Literacy Education* 12 (2): 9–32.
Creswell, J. W. 2012. *Qualitative Inquiry and Research Design: Choosing among Five Approaches*. Thousand Oaks, CA: Sage.
David, E. R. J. 2013. *Brown Skin, White Minds: Filipino-/American Postcolonial Psychology*. Charlotte, NC: Information Age.
Delpit, L., and J. K. Dowdy (Eds.). 2008. *The Skin That We Speak: Thoughts on Language and Culture in the Classroom*. New York: The New Press.
García, E., M. B. Arias, N. J. Harris Murri, and C. Serna. 2010. "Developing Responsive Teachers: A Challenge for a Demographic Reality." *Journal of Teacher Education* 61 (1–2): 132–42.
Gay, G. 2010. *Culturally Responsive Teaching: Theory, Research, and Practice*. 2nd ed. New York: Teachers College Press.
Ladson-Billings, G. 2004. "Landing on the Wrong Note: The Price We Paid for Brown." *Educational Researcher* 33 (7): 3–13.
Ladson-Billings, G. 2014. "Culturally Relevant Pedagogy 2.0: A.k.a the Remix." *Harvard Educational Review* 84 (1): 74–84.
Lee, S. J. 2015. *Unraveling the "Model Minority" Stereotype: Listening to Asian American Youth*. New York: Teachers College Press.
Nieto, S. 2013. *Finding Joy in Teaching Students of Diverse Backgrounds: Culturally Responsive and Socially Just Practices in U.S. Classrooms*. Portsmouth, NH: Heinemann.
Sensoy, O., and R. DiAngelo. 2012. *Is Everyone Really Equal? An Introduction to Key Concepts in Social Justice Education*. New York: Teachers College Press.
Shagoury, R., and B. M. Power. 2012. *Living the Questions: A Guide for Teacher-Researchers*. Portsmouth, NH: Stenhouse.
Sleeter, C. E. 2012. "Confronting the Marginalization of Culturally Responsive Pedagogy." *Urban Education* 47 (3): 562–84.
"Voices: Have You Ever Had a 'Lunch Box Moment'?" 2016, May 03. Retrieved from https://www.nbcnews.com/news/asian-america/voices-have-you-ever-had-lunch-box-moment-n566411.
Yoshino, K. 2007. *Covering: The Hidden Assault on Our Civil Rights*. New York: Random House.

5

CULTURALLY RESPONSIVE PEDAGOGY FOR IMMIGRANT STUDENTS

Xiaodi Zhou and Danling Fu

Aaden was taken to be a child soldier when he was nine after his parents were killed along with many others from his village in Somalia. Three years later he was rescued by a Red Cross team and lived in a refugee camp for another year. Currently he lives with his adopted mother in Minneapolis and goes to the local high school as a seventh grader. This is his first school experience in his life. When he began his school in the United States, he had to learn how to hold a pen, sit and listen to a teacher, and raise his hand when he wanted to leave the classroom. Often he still has nightmares of being in the war, of killing, fighting, and shooting as a child soldier; and some nights, he screams to wake himself up. He has a hard time trusting anyone, though he knows his adopted mother loves and cares about him a lot. He sees a counselor regularly for his post-traumatic stress. He is in a self-contained ESL class with twenty-two students from different countries. He began to speak some English and learned to say "hi" in different languages to his classmates.

Cha, a Hmong girl from Laos, came to this country two years ago after living in a refugee camp for six years. Now she is twelve. Her father was taken to a re-education camp in Laos before she was born, and she met her father for the first time when she was eight. She grew up in a Thai refugee camp and had all her formal schooling there before coming to the United States. Now she lives with her parents and a three-year old brother in Wisconsin. Her father works in a dairy factory, from 7:00 a.m. to

7:00 p.m. every day. When Cha gets home from school, her mother leaves to clean people's houses, and Cha takes care of her little brother and cooks dinner for the family. Only after her mother gets home around 9:00 or 10:00 p.m. can she do her homework. Her favorite time of the year is to attend their Hmong community's water festival in April, when her parents would take a day off and all the people would wear their traditional clothes and share their traditional homecooked food, singing, dancing, splashing water with each other, and getting soaked wet with joy and laugher.

Maria was in her mother's tummy when her mother trekked across the Mexican–U.S. border to come to this country. Though she is a U.S.-born Mexican American, she grows up with constant worries that her undocumented parents would be deported back to Mexico some day, a place she has only heard about but never been to. She is thirteen now, living with her mother, stepfather, and four siblings, who are eight, five, three, and one years old, in Houston, Texas. She speaks Spanish at home and in her community. As the most fluent English speaker at home, she translates for her parents and contacts the landlord and food banks for the family. She functions as a second mother to her sisters and brothers, caring and disciplining them. She loves her school and reads and writes whenever she has a quiet moment by herself. Her dream is to become a civil rights attorney when she grows up, so she can fight for the people like her parents.

Linhua was born in the United States and then sent to China to be raised by her grandparents when she was just three months old. She returned to the United States to be with her parents when she was eight. She misses her grandparents every day, and it was very hard to leave them and begin her life with parents of whom she had no memory. She doesn't like to live in their small apartment in Brooklyn, New York, and misses the green hills, rice paddies, and vegetable gardens of her hometown, especially all the exciting holidays in China: Spring Festival, Lantern Festival, Mid-Autumn Festival, Dragon Boat Festival, and so on. In addition, her parents work long hours in a restaurant every day, and she can see them only when they are back from their work around 10:00 p.m. She has learned to take care of herself in the United States, doing her homework in the afterschool program, and then walking home and heating up the food her parents brought from the restaurant for dinner. But she talks to her grandparents from her iPhone every day, which is her favorite time every night before she goes to bed. She loves school and has made quite a few friends with classmates who live in the same neighborhood. She doesn't like holidays or breaks as she feels lonely by herself at home. She loves her teacher in her self-contained bilingual class and wants to be a teacher just like her when she grows up.

These are some of the children, immigrants themselves or hailing from immigrant families, who attend our schools. Among 4.5 million students of immigrants in our public K–12 schools, over 50 percent were born in the United States, and they are not just concentrated in gateway areas but also live in urban and rural areas across the nation (NCES 2017). Our schools are becoming ever more diverse in the twenty-first century, and many classrooms are now minority majority or "new mainstream" with different cultural, linguistic, social, and life experiences.

With the increase of immigration from nations in Latin America, Asia, and Africa (Zong and Batalova 2017), immigrant students today bring with them very different heritage language fluencies, cultural knowledge, and life experiences into today's classroom. With this demographic shift, instructional considerations shift as well. While the majority of immigrants in the past have come from Europe, today's immigrants are of different colors, ethnicities, and cultures from the dominant U.S. culture.

Specifically, because today's immigrant students come from different cultural backgrounds than the Western world, U.S. classrooms need to be more open to culturally inclusive and responsive pedagogy that addresses the diverse needs of our students. For many students, current schooling experiences are subtractive in terms of their native cultures and native proficiencies, and they do not see their personal familial experiences as equally valid in the classrooms. They are prone to losing their heritage voice, suppressing their emotions, and feeling forced to acquire either a new way of expressing themselves or be treated as robot-like empty vessels.

One solution is culturally responsive pedagogy (CRP), which strives to be receptive to the diverse ways of thinking our students exhibit (Villegas and Lucas 2002). Culturally responsive pedagogy has been defined as an inclusive pedagogical approach that develops from an awareness and appreciation of the diversity inside the classroom. There are multiple needs for instructors to be culturally responsive with their students:

1. *Sociocultural Consciousness*: Understanding people's ways of thinking, behaving, and existing is deeply influenced by such factors as race/ethnicity, socioeconomic class, gender, sexuality, language fluency, and lived experience.
2. *Affirming Attitude toward Diversity*: Validating the distinct heritage and stories that minority immigrant students bring, regardless of the color of their skin, the language they speak, how much money their families have, or in what kind of environments they were raised or grew up.
3. *Commitment and Skills to Act as Agents of Change*: Moral responsibilities that teachers have in facilitating students' growth and development as conscientious and agentive human beings in the twenty-first century. Students are aware of the inequities in the world and think of creative solutions.
4. *Constructivist Views of Learning*: Students make use of prior knowledge by integrating new learning to build upon their knowledge base. This is contrary to the traditional "empty vessel" analogy and sees students as constantly making meaning and revising and building upon prior concepts. Teachers can adjust instruction to cater to the diverse resources students bring.
5. *Translanguaging Practice:* Teachers systematically create space and opportunities in their classrooms to allow students with diverse linguistic backgrounds choice of languages to maximize their potential in their school learning along with their English-proficient peers.
6. *Learning about Students*: Teachers try to understand students' personal or family funds of knowledge and experiences. This can lead to insights concerning how students live and learn, and provide reasoning into difficulties or strengths students may have. Learning about students' lives can engender empathy and bolster understanding.
7. *Culturally Responsive Teaching Practices*: Teachers create classroom environments where students are encouraged to share and express themselves, constructing their own learning, instead of rote

memorizations. Embedding inquiry initiated by students help them internalize and take ownership of their own education.

With these considerations, teachers in today's classrooms can be open and receptive to the diverse ways and means students represent their learning. Immigrant students' home resources and personal experiences can be presented in class to assist with the education of mainstream classmates.

Being culturally responsive necessitates a level of cultural empathy and historical understanding. Not all cultures have had the same experiences, nor are they privileged the same in U.S. society. Part of developing a *sociocultural consciousness* is being aware of the historical and contextual factors that have led to present conditions. It is important for students to realize that we do not exist in a vacuum, and there are multiple factors of oppression, both historical and current, that weigh on the success of immigrant students, including their documentation status, nations of origin, heritage language, religion, socioeconomic class, lived experience, and family makeup.

So, cultural responsiveness entails multiple ways of teaching, of differentiating instruction to account for the many factors that influence the learning of our immigrant students. As teachers we need to model acceptance by valuing the diverse stories of students who are different, culturally, linguistically, ethnically, socially, and economically. "Cultural responsive teaching evolved as a method for promoting 'the academic achievement and cultural competence of students of color as well as to support the abilities to critique power relations and promote equality and social justice'" (Reece and Nodine 2014, 259) and is increasingly essential in today's classrooms.

Such instruction also necessitates a more active role for both learner and instructor, to take more of an initiative in the education process. Students can actively participate in their education as they learn about more participatory forms of knowing, while teachers actively strive to understand their students and also provide a context that is open and welcoming to the diverse stories students bring to the classroom. Such mutual participation of student and teacher creates a synergy, an encounter, wherein learning and growth is fostered.

GETTING TO KNOW STUDENTS

For teachers to understand their students there can be opportunities for self-expression and divulging of personal and familial narratives. There can be *family dialogue journals* where there are direct written exchanges between pupil and instructor that allow communication to be unhindered by the judgement of classmates and social scrutiny (Allen et al. 2014). Students can share with teachers personal facets of themselves, and teachers can share their own reactions and their own stories. Through this course of sharing, a mutual understanding and connection can be nurtured. Family members can participate as well and join in the dialogic exchange, bridging school and home.

The geographical regions where the students live impact their sense of identity and may also influence their living standard and access to amenities conducive to their education. The region may also subscribe to a particular heritage language or cultural orientation. These factors influence both what the students bring to the classroom and how the material learned in school is synthesized once the child is home. For immigrant students of different heritages, this encounter of diverse cultures and languages brings a dialogic encounter between the home and the classroom that engenders novel ways of thinking that may include elements of each culture.

For example, when discussing Halloween in the U.S. classroom, a Mexican American student may bring up Día de los Muertos, a celebration in Mexico that views the dead in a more jovial, lighthearted way. Deceased family members are honored and welcomed back to join the living in vibrant displays. Skulls and skeletons have colorful, flowery attires that bring a celebratory upbeat dimension to honor death. This foreign cultural attitude can contrast with Halloween's more somber, melancholy mood that cultivates fear of the dead, whose haunts incite dread in the living.

Another issue that affects schools nowadays is the preponderance of white female teachers, who may not always be as susceptible to the experiences of other minority groups, as "98 percent of the undergraduate interns . . . are white" (Reece and Nodine 2014, 264). Many of these teachers avoid bringing up the issue of race for fear of upsetting students. But ignoring these discussions does not dispel the factors necessitating them, as they still exist in the minds of many students as unspoken forms of anxiety. As teachers, we need to be more inviting of students' diverse voices.

Students need to talk with peers and with teachers about issues that are pertinent to their lives. In this chapter, we will discuss in depth the top category of immigrant students in our classrooms today and how culturally responsive pedagogy may look with respects to their lives. Mexican immigrant students are highlighted as an example. A specific Mexican context is presented from the region that harbors a growing number of emigrants to the United States, and the U.S. locale described is one of the top destinations for these migrants. Specific cultural and linguistic factors affecting their overall educational success and experiences will be discussed.

MICHOACÁN IMMIGRANTS TO NORTH GEORGIA

We will take a closer look at the experiences of Mexican immigrant students in the United States. Not all Mexican immigration is undocumented, and in recent times, contrary to popular perceptions, the net flow of Mexican migrants has actually been in reverse, with more migrants returning to Mexico in recent years (Jordan 2015). Many Mexican immigrants to the United States have moved from the border regions to the southeastern United States. Food processing and textile industries in the rural Southeast have become economic attractions for migrants from Mexico, and specifically from the Michoacán region (Marrow 2011). Among these immigrants, many are undocumented and must work extra jobs in order to provide for their families. Their children grow up speaking Spanish and enter into a new linguistic and cultural context as they enter majority culture public schools.

The poultry processing and textile industries of North Georgia and the construction sectors of North Carolina have in recent years come to depend on the cheap and dependable contributions of Mexican labor. These migrants from Michoacán likely came to this country with the assistance of *coyotes*, or hired smugglers with local ties to the Mexican communities they serve, aboard cargo freights known as *The Beast* and endured countless hardships on their trek. Stories of their crossover, along with heritage folklore and traditions, are frequently passed on to their children in Spanish, and these children often bring these narratives in their heritage languages with them to the mainstream classroom.

Here in the States, these families may live in isolated communities across the Southeast. Their children go to school with mainstream peers, being exposed to the same curricular and popular culture artifacts. However, their learning experiences differ from others given the cultural and linguistic foundations of their lives. As teachers, we need to get to know these students' lived realities, their home languages, perhaps in ways that incorporate descriptions of family get-togethers with authentic dialogue. In describing heritage activities, new terms or novel objects may be articulated for the class so that classmates and teachers can learn another culture as well.

Being culturally responsive to children from such families can entail understanding and welcoming indigenous legends, such as the stories of *La Llorona* or *La Malinche*, tales that combine patriotism and native Mexican pride with colonial themes of treachery and betrayal. For example, the story of La Llorona, or the Weeping Woman, involves one Mexican woman who drowned her children in a lake to be with the Spanish man whom she loved. But, after that man rejected her love, in her grief she drowned herself in the same lake. At the gates of Heaven, La Llorona is stopped and made to search the lake for the souls of her children before entering. So today, near that lake, one can still hear her wails of "Mis hijos! [My children!]."

Additionally, religion is another cultural factor that needs consideration. Just because many of these students are Catholic does not mean their faith is the same as U.S. Catholics. Many Mexicans worship the *Virgen de Guadalupe*, a Mexican version of the Virgin Mary who appeared before a local peasant, Juan Diego. Many Mexican American families display a plaque or mural of this Virgin, a symbol of their indigenous Mexican spirituality. Their spiritual narratives thus differ with Catholics in the United States. Being culturally responsive may also entail recognizing the uniqueness of students' spiritual beliefs.

Thus, children are apt to come into our classrooms with such heritage narratives that may inspire their writing or impact their reading of mainstream texts. With such diverse cultural narratives, their views of the world, of how families should behave, about maternal sacrifice and Christianity elements, all influence and impact the cultural understanding of Mexican students. Being culturally responsive in the classroom means being sensitive to their perilous family narratives and to their fears of family separation, to the socioeconomic realities for these families and to their legal or documentation statuses. Being cognizant of these factors can impact and facilitate how we interact with them and how we educate them.

In Our Classrooms

A big part of one's culture is the language she or he speaks. These children of Mexican families come to school needing to learn a new language, English, as well as a new cultural context and unfamiliar ways of learning in a U.S. classroom. Often times, many of these students have not had much exposure to English, as their families are for the most part monolingual Spanish speakers. They watch Mexican television stations and many listen to Mexican Ranchera and Mariachi music. They celebrate traditional Mexican holidays with their communities, such as Día de los Muertos, Día de los Reyes Magos, La Posada, and Cinco de Mayo. They listen to ancestral narratives and stories of their parents' childhoods in Mexico, schemas that do not segue with mainstream classroom discussions in terms of both themes and language.

As a result, many of these Mexican American students may feel like they must conform to the mainstream U.S. narrative and forget their own stories in order to succeed. There may be disconnect between their home and school realities. They may not feel as if their heritage language or stories matter in the U.S. classroom. By being more accepting and welcoming of these stories, the culturally responsive educator validates these cultural truths and their home language as important facets of their identity. Diversity and multiple perspectives are valued as unique aspects of the global, interconnected world, especially in the United States, where foreign immigration has been bringing diverse cultures and languages together ever since the seventeenth century.

When in class, these students may feel more comfortable with other Mexican American classmates, with whom they share a common experience. There may be more linguistic and cultural familiarity. Thus, social and academic partitioning can occur, where the academic experiences of Mexican American students diverge from the mainstream. One possible solution is having students compose and share *home language narratives* wherein students write about a family activity and record or recreate the speech of family members in their original vernacular, in these cases Spanish.

When Mexican American students are able to share these stories and these voices with the class, classmates become privy to a different culture, to a different language, to a different way of naming the world. The language we speak captures more than the means by which we communicate, but may also express different definitions of words and different tones of communication. For example, when speaking of the bordered territory between Mexico and the United States, Mexican families refer to this land as *la frontera*. *La frontera* has two meanings: one meaning the border and the other meaning the frontier. So, *la frontera* could mean either the boundary partitioning the United States and Mexico from the perspective of some, or the frontier foretelling a new life from the perspective of others.

Students can use literacy to construct their definition of the world, with their own home languages, and construct a tone that differs from the majority culture. Utilizing different languages in the context of heritage activities and celebrations, framing language within its sociopolitical positioning, these students can incorporate elements of their heritage culture that transacts and affects, while being affected by, the mainstream culture.

For teachers, being culturally responsive in the classroom necessitates viewing students from the perspective they see themselves, not how we wish them to be. Cultural responsive pedagogy entails instructors positioning students as actors in their lives, as participants of the cultural dialogue that has characterized, and still continues to characterize, the U.S. narrative. When students' family cultures converse with the majority context, and vice versa, students and majority classmates alike are introduced to cultural dynamics in real time, situated in the lived context of their world.

When students are asked to compose *home language narratives*, they can also introduce their heritage cultures with mainstream classmates. They can lead a lesson to the class about their culture. Activities can include the following:

1. Share and discuss photos of their family heritage celebrations and traditions

2. Share a story, folktale, or legend that is indigenous to their heritage culture
3. Talk about a trip to their heritage nation
4. Model some traditional attire
5. Share some of the heritage meals, customs, or foods
6. Teach the class how to speak their heritage language

In addition to introducing their home culture, they may also introduce another foreign culture. One activity paired with the *home language narrative* activity could be for students to introduce a new culture apart from their own. This could be a *cultural introduction* activity. Some sample activities or questions may include the following:

1. Research this culture, about its traditions, stories, and customs to teach them to the class
2. Talk a little about the history and geography of the culture
3. Bring a poster, a cultural object, or show a video that has significance for the culture
4. Highlight one city, one holiday, or one famous person from that culture
5. If you were a travel agent, how would you advertise or convince potential travelers to visit?
6. How is the culture viewed in the United States or the world?

This activity gives immigrant students a chance to learn about another culture, about its characteristics. For example, Mexican American students can learn about the experiences and culture of Egypt, about its ancestry and fabled past, and share it with the class.

In researching another culture, minority students learn to view culture as a universal and ubiquitous aspect of all of us. They learn to understand and empathize with other cultural perspectives. In teaching about this new culture, they can internalize that culture, share its stories, and feel empowered to be experts. In such ways, they may also not feel as different and excluded from the mainstream, when they learn to see all cultures as having unique characteristics different from each other.

It is important to remember with these cultural activities to give classmates sufficient time to respond and react to the presentation. Students need ample time to process by themselves and with each other the new information they are acquiring and make sense of the material within their own cultural schema. Through interaction with classmates, these students also participate in negotiation of definitions and the relativism of cultural notions. Being culturally responsive means being aware of the cultural relativism within the world and knowing how best to conceive of each culture.

As the leaders of tomorrow, today's students live in an increasingly systemic, interconnected world. They are exposed to an ever-growing number of different cultures and languages in their daily lives. While we are culturally responsive in our instruction, they need this skill more than ever to negotiate an ever more interconnected society. One of the most important skills to have in this new world is a deeper empathy and appreciation for those different from us. When immigrant students are taught that same empathy for others, they gain insight into how their own culture may be viewed by the mainstream culture as well, and this can temper their own experiences within the majority culture.

The goal of culturally responsive classrooms is not to diminish the uniqueness of our immigrant students, or even to showcase their difference from the mainstream and highlight the hardship of their lives, nor to make them synthetically feel as if they are "American." Rather, the goal is to value that difference and to reframe their points of contrast as positives. Such contexts nurture appreciation for one's own and other cultures, to encourage students to view themselves and each other as important carriers of storied pasts, to find pride in those stories. In such ways, classrooms can mirror the current globalization trends in the world, already manifested by our ever-diversifying schools.

CONCLUSION

In today's society, teachers increasingly need to develop culturally responsive ways to engage with their students. Learning to view the different cultures of students not as an impediment but as a resource is crucial in today's classrooms. The reality that we have diverse students nowadays gives us a rich palette with which to work to paint our vibrant instruction. Not only do we value their differences with words, but we can also encourage their own presentation and assertion of their heritage selves.

Being culturally responsive means attending to the differences in our classrooms. These differences are what make us stronger, in our ability to view situations from various cultural perspectives, and to name them with disparate languages. Being culturally responsive does not mean to ignore mainstream students, especially those with European heritage, that somehow they do not have any culture besides the "American" culture. Teachers can put forth the notion that all people have unique cultures, to even encourage mainstream students to research their own unique heritages and European ancestries.

By pointing out the differences and diversity in our classrooms, and of the connections, we incite a larger discussion regarding culture itself. Culture can be an idea that separates us, that categorizes and partitions us into segments for others to recognize and justify our appearances or behaviors. But, given the numerous connections and intersections of cultures, we can even conclude with our students that rigid notions of culture can separate us, but our common humanity conjoins us. We use distinct languages and different words to characterize the same emotions, the same thoughts, and the same expressions. Culturally responsive instruction can not only differentiate teaching, it can also teach the commonality that tethers all students to a colorful human world.

SUGGESTIONS TO GAIN FIRST-HAND KNOWLEDGE IN BECOMING CULTURAL RESPONSIVE TEACHERS

- Learn about the countries and regions where your immigrant students come from.
- Interview students who are immigrants or from immigrant families to gain first-hand knowledge of their living and immigration experience.
- Interview students whose parents and relatives are undocumented immigrants to gain an understanding of their views and positions in their current situations.
- Visit communities, churches, or neighborhood of residents of your immigrant students or their families to understand their cultures and current living situations.
- Read books or narratives by cultural insiders to provide glimpses into the distinct lived realities immigrant students potentially experience.

• Learn some greeting words from the countries your students and their families came from to show your interest in their heritage and backgrounds.

REFERENCES

Allen, J., J. Beaty, A. Dean, J. Jones, S. S. Mathews, J. McCreight, A. M. Simmons, and E. Schwedler. 2014. *Family Dialogue Journals: School-Home Partnerships That Support Student Learning*. New York: Teachers College Press.

Jordan, M. 2015 (November 19). "Mexican Immigration to the U.S. Reverses." *The Wall Street Journal*. Retrieved from https://www.wsj.com/articles/mexican-immigration-to-u-s-reverses-1447954334.

Marrow, H. B. 2011. *New Destination Dreaming: Immigration, Race, and Legal Status in the Rural American South*. Stanford, CA: Stanford University Press.

National Center for Education Statistics [NCES]. 2017. "The Condition of Education 2017 (2017-144), English Language Learners in Public Schools." Retrieved from https://nces.ed.gov/programs/coe/indicator_cgf.asp.

Reece, L., and P. Nodine. 2014. "When Immigrant Is Synonymous with Terrorist: Culturally Responsive Teaching with English Learners." *The Social Studies* 105 (6): 259–65.

Villegas, A. M., and T. Lucas. 2002. "Preparing Culturally Responsive Teachers Rethinking the Curriculum." *Journal of Teacher Education* 53 (1): 20–32.

Zong, J., and J. Batalova. 2017. "Frequently Requested Data on Immigrants and Immigration in the United States." *Migration Policy Institute*. Retrieved from http://www.migrationpolicy.org.

Section II

Reflection and Advocacy

6

NEWCOMERS AMONG US

Teachers Creating an Inclusive Classroom Haven
for Immigrant Students

Ruth McKoy Lowery, Cheryl Logan, and Deandra J. McKoy

At a professional development workshop for teachers, Ruth (one of the authors of this chapter) presented her research on the challenges many Caribbean immigrant students and their parents face as they acclimate to the American school system. One teacher approached her after the workshop and said simply, "thank you." She further explained that she had a student from the Caribbean in her fourth-grade classroom, and he was struggling. She wondered if his difficulty was more about "accent" and word usage than it was about "language." Her school, however, would not authorize testing services since he was from an English-speaking country. He did not qualify for ELL [English-language learner] services. How could she help this student succeed in her classroom?

A move toward a global economy has prompted greater opportunities and motivations for cross-cultural exchanges and border crossings than ever before. Consequently, more and more immigrants are crossing borders, creating the need for cultural understanding and acceptance of various nations and ethnicities within the United States. There is a need for teachers and teacher educators to understand immigrant children entering our classrooms, as we create a space for them to share and practice their cultural beliefs, mores, and heritage.

The opening epigraph confirms this concept. The belief that good teachers, teachers who are culturally responsive to the needs of the students they teach, work to produce a classroom environment where their students can learn. Bajaj and Suresh (2018) suggested that when schools become havens for students, their paths to a better life show greater promise. In the remainder of this chapter, we communicate the experiences of two teacher educators (Ruth and Cheryl) and one elementary classroom teacher (Deandra) and our work toward creating havens for the diverse students we encounter in our classrooms. We share examples of breaking down barriers as we advocate for safe classroom spaces for all students. As we learn to embrace the changes in our global society, we also celebrate the unique qualities and the different experiences a diverse student body brings to U.S. classrooms.

THE CHANGING LANDSCAPE OF IMMIGRATION

There is a heartfelt cry for a pluralistic society—a society where immigrants can maintain their identities, cultural values, beliefs, and heritage while simultaneously working to achieve an American dream of liberty and justice for all. One important space where we should begin to make a shift in this direction is within our classrooms. We must shift our pedagogical mindset from being teachers whose practices only reinforce the dominant culture and discourse that encourages total assimilation to be teachers who are more critical and acknowledge the diverse experiences our students bring to our classrooms. Teachers need to celebrate the value and benefit of these differences in our students as we work to engender a common classroom culture, one where all students feel that they belong.

Grobman (2007) encourages teachers to become critical multiculturalists. Critical multiculturalists undertake pedagogical practices that move us away from "othering" difference and employ practices that recognize and embrace difference because of its value for all. These teachers place difference at the center of their practice by acknowledging and confronting practices that have a long history of being "used as . . . exclusionary and oppressive practices" (Grobman 2007, xiii). They work to institute practices that meet children where they are and then build on those experiences to move them to the next level.

CULTURALLY RELEVANT TEACHING AND TEACHER ADVOCACY

In the last three decades, educators have engaged in discussions about meeting the needs of students, especially underachieving students. Gloria Ladson-Billings (1995) argued for a culturally relevant perspective because of the "growing disparity between the racial, ethnic, and cultural characteristics of teachers and students along with the continued academic failure of African American, Native American and Latino students" (483). Gay (2013) furthers this notion by explicating for culturally responsive teaching, teaching which focuses on the needs of the whole students.

Culturally responsive teaching is instruction that uses "the heritages, experiences, and perspectives of different ethnic and racial groups to teach students who are members of them more effectively" (Gay 2015, 124). In order for teachers to be culturally responsive in their teaching, they must educate themselves about the cultures, customs, beliefs, and values of the students they teach. Taking the initiative and time to learn about the values, customs, and heritage of the students in our classrooms sends a message to students and their families that we recognize and value their lives and that we care.

Culturally relevant teaching cultivates trusting relationships that foster environments where students are willing to learn from teachers. If immigrant students feel that teachers genuinely care about them and are interested in their success, they will rise to perform high levels of academic success for us; and on the contrary, if they perceive that we don't care, they won't learn from us. In many ethnic groups, students strive to succeed in order to please their teachers only when they feel teachers genuinely care for them.

Teacher Beliefs

One of the most important premises of culturally responsive teaching is teacher beliefs. Gay (2015) noted that teacher beliefs about students' "ethnic, racial, and cultural diversity determine their instructional behaviors" (126). For example, teachers who have deficit beliefs about immigrant children's academic aptitudes and social and moral behaviors will provide students with instruction at the knowledge and comprehension levels because they do not believe these students are capable of higher levels of thinking and learning such as application, analysis, synthesis, or evaluation.

Similarly, teachers implement activities and strategies in their classroom to control student behavior because they do not believe these students are capable of exercising self-control and sound moral and ethical judgment. On the contrary, culturally responsive teaching requires teachers to have high expectations for immigrant students and to see them as capable, high achievers rather than seeing them from a deficit perspective. Consequently, culturally responsive teachers create learning environments that are academically rigorous, exciting, and cooperative for all students.

Culturally responsive teaching acknowledges the fact that immigrant students do not come to the U.S. classroom as empty slates. Teachers acknowledge and honor the funds of knowledge that immigrant students bring with them to the learning environment (Yosso 2005). They recognize that the children and their families bring a wealth of expert knowledge, lived experiences, and heritage that can be beneficial to all. In the remainder of this chapter, we share examples from our classrooms to highlight how we enact culturally responsive teaching perspectives with our students.

CHERYL'S CLASSROOM

As teacher educators and classroom teachers, we often find our classroom a fertile ground for nurturing a diverse student body. The procedures, rules, and curriculum instituted in teacher education spaces can and should prepare teachers to be lifelong learners. Here, I share one strategy I use to help preservice teachers begin to reflect on why and how to become culturally responsive educators through a lesson on cultural identity.

We begin by reflecting on our own heritage, cultural practices, values, and beliefs. Using a cultural web (Buckelew and Fishman 2011), I ask preservice teachers in my diversity class to think about their cultural identities through several categories, for example, education, geography, religion, family status, and race/ethnicity. They look internally or communicate with family members to help them reflect on experiences they had related to these topics.

After the preservice teachers have had time to compose and reflect on their cultural identities, I ask them to share their webs in small groups. I bring them back together and ask them to share what they noticed about what they heard from their peers. They often comment that they have been taking classes together for three to four years, yet there were things they did not know about one another.

The preservice teachers expressed gratitude for the assignment and opportunity to share because they felt a greater appreciation and respect for one another from their shared cultural identity webs. Although 99 percent of them identified as white, middle class, Christian, and heterosexual, there were vast differences in the stories and information they shared, and these differences enabled them to have a greater appreciation and respect for one another.

From this activity, I share about the power that lies in acknowledging difference and creating space for difference to be celebrated and embraced rather than to isolate, divide, or oppress. The cultural web assignment was instrumental in creating the space to facilitate a sense of cultural pride and identity while simultaneously embracing and valuing others who shared their different educational and childhood backgrounds.

Being Authentic about Culturally Relevant Teaching

I share my pedagogical stance as a critical educator as I push my preservice teachers to have uncomfortable experiences that position them as the "other," for example, attending local Black, Korean, and Jewish religious services. Other activities include having them view online videos of stories from around the world, watch TED Talks, and read current news. I incorporate the activities to help them experience other people's values and beliefs that are different from theirs and to empathize with differences all around us.

The preservice teachers share that they do feel like an "outsider" as they participate in these activities because the experiences are so different from their lived realities. I use this teachable experience to ask them to consider what could have been done in those settings to make them feel more included, valued, and respected because of their difference rather than be isolated because of it. This leads to a discussion of the changing demographics of our country and how these changes have affected the demographics of our classrooms bringing in immigrant children whose heritage, cultural values, and behaviors are different from the values, morals, and behaviors of the dominant culture here in the United States.

Our job as educators is to find ways to help preservice teachers prepare for the diverse classrooms they will undoubtedly teach in as the student population continues to change to a more racially diverse student body. Learning about the various cultures and customs within the classroom also provides teachers with information that can help them design lessons and instruction that will meet the learning styles of the students within their classrooms. This is especially important for immigrant populations. Connecting lessons to students' ethnic and cultural learning styles ensures students' academic success and conveys positive messages to students about their identities and cultural heritage.

DEANDRA'S CLASSROOM

Being a culturally responsive teacher is immensely important for my students' academic and social-emotional growth and success when working with a diverse group of students. I understand that my students learn differently, and I cannot ignore their cultures and socioeconomic backgrounds. In my classroom, I practice an inclusive environment by developing positive relationship with my students, providing them with what they need in order to succeed. I also work hard to develop a positive working relationship with their parents by keeping them informed about our weekly activities.

Creating a positive relationship with my students is essential. Their home life may be in upheaval, but when they enter the walls of my classroom, I want them to know that they are in a safe environment where they are wanted and cared for. The school environment for some students, especially my immigrant and culturally diverse students, may be in complete contrast to experiences they had in other school settings. This can be quite daunting for them.

Being Authentic about Culturally Relevant Teaching

One way of fostering positive relationships is through morning meetings (Kriete and Davis 2014). Our meetings consist of greeting, sharing, a brief activity, and a message. In the mornings, we gather around the rug, and students greet each other by name. The students learn how to greet each other respectfully. They learn to pronounce each other's names properly and to wait their turn at speaking or presenting. After our greeting, students get an opportunity to share something that is important or significant to them. This varies from "I learned how to ride a bike" to "my grandmother is visiting from China." Throughout the academic year, they learn fun and engaging ways to greet each other, which they love.

One school year, I had a Muslim student, Karim (pseudonym), whose family emigrated from Jordan. His family consisted of his parents and his three siblings. With English being his second language, there was a language communication gap. My main communication was with Karim's father because his mother spoke very limited English. Karim's father was available to meet only on Mondays because of his work schedule. Like many families, his parents were concerned about his academic progress. We developed a progress-monitoring plan to help him improve academically.

Socially and emotionally, Karim thrived in our classroom. During Ramadan, he observed the traditional fast, and many of the class did not understand why he was not eating lunch but spent lunchtime in the media center. I read *Lailah's Lunchbox: A Ramadan Story* (2015) by Reem Faruqi to the class. The story helped the class to get a better understanding of why Karim fasted for the holiday. He was also able to relate to the story. Each time we read a book about diverse cultures, we locate the country on the map so students receive a visual of each location in comparison to where we live.

Another student was Peng, whose family emigrated from China. Unlike Karim, Peng was born in the United States but spoke Chinese at home. At home, he used his native Chinese name but used an English name at school. Like Karim, it was difficult to schedule conferences with Peng's parents because of their work schedule. However, I made sure that I was flexible, and they could reach me by phone if needed. Because Peng's mother spoke very limited English and relied on her son to translate, I used handouts as visual aids with short and concise wording to communicate any important information with her. She read English but was not as confident in her verbal communication. I ensured that she had the materials so she could communicate with her husband at home.

Incorporating multicultural literature in my classroom reading is an important way for me to immerse students in learning about diverse cultures. Having two immigrant students made it all the more necessary, as I wanted all students to feel like they belonged. Reading several stories about different cultures normalized the experience for them. It gave my students the opportunity as readers to learn about the lifestyles of other students and/or their environments. The students learned to listen to each other, and their immigrant peers felt welcome and accepted. The greatest foundation to acceptance and tolerance is helping my students learn to respect each other. These activities allow for class community building and sends the message that our classroom is a place of respect and positive interactions.

RUTH'S CLASSROOM

Elsewhere (Lowery 2000), I shared the story of first being introduced to Rosa Guy's novel *The Friends* (1973) by an immigrant student in my fifth-grade classroom. Marian (pseudonym), who was from the West Indies, admonished me; she wanted me to read the novel because we did not "have any West Indian stories in the class library." As she ran off to play with her friends, she stopped and turned back to face me: "Miss L., since you're Jamaican, too, I thought you would like it."

The covers of the novel and several of the pages were badly torn. Flipping to the back pages, I noticed that the book was two years overdue from a high school library. I was fascinated, immediately thinking that students must find this novel rather interesting to keep it out of the library and yet in local circulation so long. My interest piqued, I began reading the novel during our silent reading session. *The Friends* chronicled the story of Phyllisia, a young West Indian girl, who immigrated with her family to Harlem during the 1960s. Phyllisia had difficulty adjusting to the change until she developed a friendship with an unlikely ally in the class, Edith. Things began to change as Phyllisia slowly learned to appreciate her friend.

I shared *The Friends* with my class that year, and while we did not have many novels available about the West Indies for fifth grade, we read stories like Newbery author Mildred D. Taylor's *Roll of Thunder, Hear My Cry* (1976). We incorporated poetry and picture books, and I quickly realized how much my students yearned to read stories about their home countries. Later as I became a teacher educator, I knew I had to introduce my preservice teachers to diverse books so they would be able to share them in their future classrooms. Over the years, the creation of diverse book awards like the Américas, Pura Belpré, and Coretta Scott King awards have made it easier to find quality award-winning diverse literature to share with preservice and practicing teachers and in K–12 curricula.

Being Authentic about Culturally Relevant Teaching

As a teacher educator, I teach children's literature courses and courses on diversity and equity in education. An activity I use with preservice teachers is the viewing and discussion of the documentary film *Paper Clips* (2004) produced by Joe Fab. The preservice teachers view the film, reflect and respond independently, discuss in small groups with their peers, and then do another independent reflection based on their small group discussion.

Paper Clips is the story about a small Tennessee town, Whitwell, where three teachers and their eighth-grade students decided to learn more about the Holocaust by collecting paper clips to represent the 6 million Jews killed by the Nazis. They ended up collecting over 25 million paperclips with donations coming from all over the world as people heard about their project. Along the way, the students, teachers, and the community at large learned so much more than they imagined; they created a permanent monument on the school grounds. Today, students from all over the country are able to visit and tour the site.

After including this activity for several semesters, it has been enlightening to see the deep conversations that result from the preservice teachers' discussions. For many, this was their first time hearing about the film. In their individual reflections, they think about how difficult it must have been to undertake this project but how fulfilling it was to see that the students were active participants who actually lead the project and saw it to completion. Several shared that it was hard to hold back the tears as they realize how hatred caused so many innocent people to die.

After the preservice teachers reflect on the film, I bring it back to more recent stories, immigrants turned away at the borders in the United States, Germany, and many countries around the world; hate crimes in schools and other spaces directed at immigrants or people who looked "different"; crises in Darfur and Somalia; and most currently, the war in Syria. Students watch the news and read all they can find online about the different topics.

We then bring it home to our classroom. How do we as teachers prepare a culturally responsive classroom for the students who will ultimately walk through our classroom doors? It is not a matter of "if they will come," but rather "when they do come, how will we meet their needs as teachers?" Overwhelmingly, the preservice teachers come away from this experience with a deeper understanding of what it means to be the teacher who makes a difference, the teacher who goes the extra mile to make all students feel like they belong, and the teacher who exhibits a culturally responsive perspective for all students.

CONCLUSION

As we share our individual experiences of working with our student populations to promote culturally responsive pedagogy in our classrooms, we realize how important it is for teacher educators, teachers, and other stakeholders to work together to create safe havens for our students, especially our immigrant and culturally diverse students. We realize too the similarities in our practices as teachers enacting culturally responsive strategies to meet the needs of our students.

One way to engage others is by focusing on the cultural customs and heritage of these students. This allows teachers and students to gain knowledge of each other, allowing us to cross borders and build bridges to understand and appreciate the unique differences and the commonalities among us. The goal should not be to force immigrant students to conform or assimilate; rather, it should be to share and celebrate in a safe space. Learning about the various cultures and customs within the classroom also provides teachers with information that can help us design lessons and instruction that will meet the learning styles of the students within our classrooms. This is especially important for immigrant and minoritized students.

REFERENCES

Bajaj, M., and S. Suresh. 2018. "The 'Warm Embrace' of a Newcomer School for Immigrant and Refugee Youth." *Theory Into Practice* 57 (2): 91–98.

Buckelew, M. B., and A. Fishman. 2011. *Reaching and Teaching Diverse Populations: Strategies for Moving Beyond Stereotypes.* Thousand Oaks, CA: Sage.

Fab, J. (Producer), and E. Berlin (Director). 2004. *Paper Clips* [Motion Picture]. United States: Miramax.

Faruqi, R., and L. Lyon (Illustrator). 2015. *Lailah's Lunchbox: A Ramadan Story.* Thomaston, ME: Tilbury House.

Gay, G. 2013. "Teaching To and Through Cultural Diversity." *Curriculum Inquiry* 43 (1): 48–70.

Gay, G. 2015. "The What, Why and How of Culturally Responsive Teaching: International Mandates, Challenges and Opportunities." *Multicultural Education Review* 7 (3): 23–139.

Grobman, L. 2007. *Multicultural Hybridity: Transforming American Literary Scholarship and Pedagogy.* Urbana, IL: National Council of Teachers of English.

Guy, R. 1973. *The Friends.* New York: Bantam Double Dell.

Kriete, R., and C. Davis. 2014. *The Morning Meeting Book K–8.* 3rd ed. Turners Falls, MA: Northeast Foundation for Children.

Ladson-Billings, G. 1995. "Toward a Theory of Culturally Relevant Pedagogy." *American Educational Research Journal* 32 (3): 465–91.

Lowery, R. M. 2000. *Immigrants in Children's Literature.* New York: Peter Lang.

Taylor, M. D. 1976. *Roll of Thunder, Hear My Cry.* New York: Dell.

Yosso, T. J. 2005. "Whose Culture Has Capital? A Critical Race Theory Discussion of Community Cultural Wealth." *Race Ethnicity and Education* 8 (1): 69–91.

7

MY LIFE AS AN IMMIGRANT IN AMERICA

Garfield Daley

I am Jamaican by birth and a U.S. citizen by naturalization. My family and I immigrated to the United States of America when I was nineteen years old. Reflecting on my youthful days in Jamaica, I can remember being immensely excited about learning and going to school. There was never a time that I can recall not being motivated to go to school. I've always had an insatiable desire to learn. That attribute in conjunction with my Jamaican roots and upbringing has immensely helped to shape who I am today as a man and a parent, even to this day, after more than twenty-six years of living in America.

Jamaica, because of its socioeconomic situation, is popularly referred to as a third-world country, and I, as a Jamaican, find this offensive. The term's roots date back to the cold war era but has since been rendered obsolete. As noted in history text books, the term originally referred to a country's allegiance to one of two world orders. "First world" meant a country was aligned with NATO and Socialism; "second world" meant allegiance to the Soviet Union and Communism; and "third world" meant allegiance to neither. Since the collapse of the Soviet Union, the term "third world" has become interchangeable with the term "developing nation" (a more politically correct term), and in simple terms this often means the country is underdeveloped.

The designation or categorization of being underdeveloped specifically refers to the country's poor infrastructure, insufficient access to proper health care, poor living conditions, its overall economic viability, and, lastly, its education level. To be fair, I do agree that my homeland is indeed underdeveloped in most if not all of those categories. However, when it comes to the level of educational attainment, I believe that Jamaica and its people are extremely misunderstood and underrated. Thus, the reason I take offense to the term as it is in my opinion a generalization, and worse, a mischaracterization of Jamaicans' intellectual overall level.

As a child traversing through the Jamaican education system, I obviously had no reference point on which to base my opinions of the importance of the education system. However, not long after immigrating to the United States, I swiftly began to recognize value in the education system I left behind. Eager to acclimate into my new home country, the United States of America, "the land of opportunity" where all you need is a dream and the will to work toward it, still thriving with a zest to learn, I remember networking with others familiar with the system in order to jump-start my post–high school education. The feedback received at the time was from some Americans as well as a mix of Jamaicans who immigrated many years prior. From all the feedback, the consensus deduced that the American school system lacked tolerance for immigrants.

To be clear, the intolerance is not solely reserved for or solely directed toward immigrants, nor is it native to or confined to the school system. However, it is rooted in a societal mindset that is deficient in empathy. Any person or group that is not of the community, locally or nationally, is usually not very well received to say the least. Therefore, with that said, immigrants, especially ones unfamiliar with this societal mindset native to the American culture on a whole, usually suffer the worse.

Twenty-eight years later and counting, I am now somewhat embroidered into the American culture and to a lesser extent, the American culture into me. Life in my new home country has been blissful for the most part and full of rewards. During this time frame, I've owned a few real estate properties. I've held three jobs, tenuring three, twelve, and twelve years each successively, with the third being my current in which I hold an upper management position. In addition, I've been blissfully married now for sixteen years, and my wife and I have two wonderful sons, ages thirteen and fourteen. Between us both we make a decent wage and are able to live comfortably, mostly by means of living a humble life that is within our means.

After reading all of that, it would be easy to surmise that life here in America for me has been nothing but a blissful journey free of obstacles. However, that is far from the truth. I have had to overcome many obstacles along the way and am still learning to navigate some to this day. Many of these obstacles were, and still are, undoubtedly linked to the fact that I am an immigrant. Moreover, I know this to be true because there have been many circumstances in which I, the immigrant person, along with other nonimmigrants in the same situation, was the only one that had to employ special maneuvers in order to circumnavigate around obstacles in my way. Many if not all of these obstacles should never be obstacles in the first place.

Obstacles and unfair biases faced by immigrants of this country (and many others I'm sure) can include accent, skin color, religion, ethnicity, socioeconomic background, and even one's ambition to succeed. I believe that how America (and the world as a whole) categorizes, views, and, frankly, looks down upon underdeveloped countries and their people, in conjunction with a lack of empathy and unwillingness to accept other groups from outside of the American culture, is directly linked to the immigrant experience.

This is often evident as immigrants try to pursue their dreams by means of immersing themselves into the American education system and work force. Again, to be clear, my claim is not that only immigrants are faced with these obstacles. However, I can attest to the fact that these obstacles are generally exponentially more prevalent and harsher among immigrants, particularly those of countries categorized as third world or the more politically correct term, underdeveloped countries.

In my current employment, I am the operations manager for the West Coast office of the Audio Visual Systems Integration Firm. Our firm takes on projects all across the United States and internationally. We are in the business of designing, building, and installing professional audio visual systems in venues such as sports arenas and stadiums, theme parks, houses of worship, and government and educational facilities. In my tenure thus far I have successfully managed myriad projects, ranging in sizes from small PA systems in local community churches to the most technologically advanced audio reinforcement AV systems found in venues such as our U.S. House of Representatives in Washington, DC.

I have also managed projects for state-of-the-art concert halls from Miami to Los Angeles, as well as theme parks across America and as far away as Japan. I joined the company starting at the very bottom as a technician. Within six months, I was made a supervisor, and within twelve months, I was made a project superintendent. Within two years, I was allotted a company car—a privilege and benefit up until then that was only extended to upper management staff.

Sometime after, I became interim operations lead after the then operations manager resigned. I remained in this position for another five or so years until I relocated to our West coast office where I am now officially the operations manager. I say "officially" as most previous promotions and titles given were never made official. In fact, while filling in as operations lead, the position of operations manager was posted and filled on three occasions, and on all three occasions I was tasked to some level to either train or guide the new hires. However, on every attempt to fill the position from the outside, the individuals hired ended up leaving for other opportunities as they were usually either underqualified or not adequately experienced in this segment of the technology industry, and/or they did not have the people management skills or qualifications to run a department such as ours.

Driven by my tenacity to succeed and my determination to always be a positive influence on my kids and my wife (along with a personal tendency to be naive at times), I've managed to maintain a positive attitude along the way even when I am consciously aware of the fact that I am being unjustly overlooked at times. I was always well-liked by my peers, my subordinates, and other management staff. Since being appointed the interim operations lead position, until present my direct report has been to the CEO. He and I have maintained a respectful relationship over the past five years that has at times seemed more like a friendship than employer and employee.

We speak candidly with each other on a regular basis about anything from business, politics, life, family, marriage, and raising our kids. He has complimented me, on multiple occasions, on my intellect, my communication skills, both verbal and written, my ability to manage people, and my ability to overcome work challenges in order to meet goals. He has even mentioned to me on occasion how some positive attributes and skillsets I possess would make me a better general manager than others currently managing some of the firm's locations.

However, with all that said, not once has those acknowledgments by him, or others in decision-making positions in the firm, translated into any real and tangible advancements for me. Recently during a conversation with him discussing some upcoming structural changes in the planning stages of being implemented within the company, such as adding some new components to the accounting department and establishing some new employee empowerment initiatives in the form of various levels of employee training, my advice and opinion were requested and I kindly obliged as always. His concern about successorship of some key management positions (one of which he has in the past stated I am qualified for) was also brought up, to which I asked what his plans were if the need to implement a successor becomes necessary. His answer was "Well, we would have to hire . . . or shut down."

I find these overlookings of my qualifications and potential, as well as those of others in my situation, to be directly linked to my status of being an immigrant. We are often relegated to lower positions and only given credibility and opportunity when those prospects are more ancillary in nature and especially so in the cases where manual labor is required. In addition, we are unfortunately given far less opportunities involving positions of power that require a certain level of professionalism and a certain level of intellect, even in cases as myself when the individual in question has already proven their loyalty and dedication, and their abilities have been on full display and even in the past acknowledged by superiors.

I am proud to be a U.S. citizen, but I am equally proud to be a Jamaican. I am an immigrant of this country, and I can't change that nor do I wish to. The change I hope for is that of the mindset of the general population of this country and all other countries that are hosts to millions of immigrants and potential immigrants from countries around the world in search of something better than their home country can provide them. Some people merely migrate in search of an education, while some migrate in search of career advancements not attainable in their home country.

Some people immigrate with the dream and hope of changing the trajectory of their family's generation, as in the case of my parents when they decided to transplant our family into the United States of America. They do this by being willing to make personal sacrifices in the face of unjust biases for the sake of granting the next generation of their family a greater potential of achieving a better life than could have been attained in their native land. In all cases, regardless of social, political, or economic categorizations of someone's homeland, I believe that each individual is born with a God-given potential to succeed. Moreover, if given a fair opportunity to explore and realize their potential, they would not only be of benefit to themselves and their families but, to a greater extent, their host country and its society.

My children are not immigrants. They do not have a Jamaican accent. They have no mannerisms that could be categorized as Jamaican or immigrant. My hope is that they will not have to face any of the challenges typical to immigrants. My goal and responsibility as their parent, still navigating the obstacle course–like nature of being a first-generation immigrant, is to learn from every lesson and transpose them into lessons I can teach my children so that they grow up to become valuable contributors to American society or whatever country they ultimately choose.

My greatest hope is that regardless of my children's roles in the future, whether as educators, students, employers, or employees, they will treat immigrants as they would have wanted their father to be treated: with dignity, with respect, and given a fair opportunity to fulfill or explore his full potential. In the end, it not only benefits the immigrant but the entire country, from an economic perspective, if nothing else.

8

THE HIDDEN COSTS OF IMMIGRATION

Ann M. Dillard

"In 2015, 17.9 million children under age 18 lived with at least one immigrant parent. They accounted for 26 percent of the 69.9 million children under age 18 in the United States." (Zong and Batalova 2017)

The National Alliance on Mental Illness (NAMI Fact Sheet) reported that one in every four children has a mental disorder. Depression is the most common disorder and accounts for one in every eight cases. This presents at a higher number for boys in childhood and girls in adolescence. Half of all mental illnesses begin by age fourteen, and three quarters are realized by age twenty-four.

Mental disorders are important risk factors for other diseases, as well as unintentional and intentional injury. Fifty percent of students age fourteen and older who are living with a mental illness drop out of high school, and 65 percent of boys and 75 percent of girls in juvenile detention have at least one mental illness. Teachers are influential forces in the lives of children. School and childcare programs consist of over 18 million children from immigrant households.

Immigration is a significant stressor that compounds mental illness in children and families. The aim of this chapter is to equip teachers with awareness and understanding of some of the challenges that immigrant children and their families face on a daily basis, with the hopes of building culturally responsive relationships.

When we think of immigrant families, it is important to remember that there are many forms of immigration and each student/family's immigration story is different from the other. There are immigrants who have legal documentation who immigrated to America for better opportunities, to make a life for themselves and their family. There are also immigrants who have gained undocumented entrance into the United States in search of a better quality of life. There are refugee immigrants who are in the United States because of humanitarian reasons. Other immigrants have been victims of war, or other governmental persecution, and immigrated in search of asylum. Each group has its own set of extenuating circumstances and needs that deserve to be addressed individually and equitably.

As a licensed marriage and family therapist who emigrated from Jamaica to the United States in 1982, I worked for over twenty years as a consultant with inner city schools, and for the past four years as a school-based mental health therapist. I have worked closely with immigrant populations to help empower students and families to navigate the school systems as well as offer individual, group, and family therapy to these populations. I provide ongoing support to educators including the authoring and delivery of professional development in the areas of mental health and cultural diversity.

While the stories shared in this chapter are real, I have changed the names and some details for confidentiality purposes. I share these stories for educational purposes with the intention of illustrating the complexities of immigrant children and their families.

CASSIE'S STORY

I am fourteen years old, the oldest of four children, and am an eighth grader at a large inner city public school. My parents work long hours at several odd jobs in order to provide for our basic needs. It is my responsibility to get my younger siblings ready for school and see them off to their school buses each day. Sometimes it is very difficult because they rarely listen to me. Lately, there has been a lot of crying and yelling between my parents. This causes my siblings to get scared, and we end up fighting each other. Sometimes I don't get to see my mother at all because she is working extra hard to save up money in case they get deported. We have been having many family meetings lately because we have to make a plan for what will happen if my parents get taken by ICE (Immigration and Customs Enforcement). If my parents are not home by a certain time, that could mean that they

> got caught and then it's up to me to put the plan in place. I think about this all the time. I'm trying to keep my grades up because my parents say that I need to become a doctor so that I can help take care of my family. It's been hard because I can't concentrate, and I cry a lot during school. I don't get to hang out with my friends anymore. Lately I've been cutting myself because it feels good while I'm doing it, but then I get embarrassed. My teachers are starting to get on my nerves.

The threat of deportation is real for our students, especially in this current political climate. It is important to know that even though the Latino population is the fastest-growing population in our country, children from other cultural groups face similar immigration issues and the possibility of deportation of their parents. The constant worry of their family being separated is one that is common in many immigrant populations. Children who are born in the United States to undocumented parents live with the constant fear of having to move to a country that is unfamiliar to them in order to keep their family together.

In this scenario, Cassie's responsibilities are insurmountable. She is facing significant toxic stress and anxiety. She is seeking relief through self-harming behaviors. Cutting is a non-suicidal, self-harming method that is common among adolescents who do not have the appropriate skills to manage their overwhelming anxiety and feelings of powerlessness. Their intention is not to die, but rather to gain instant relief and distraction from their emotional pain. Her teachers might overlook Cassie because she is a high achiever and does not present behavioral challenges at school.

Building a trusting relationship with Cassie could provide an outlet for her to gain tools and other resources to navigate her challenges. Teachers sometimes become overwhelmed when they learn about the challenges their students face. It is important that teachers remember that they are not being asked or are not expected to rescue or save their students. Directing them to resources and being a consistent trusting adult in their lives helps alleviate some of these stresses.

AKIEM'S STORY

Akiem is a nine-year-old boy who started school in the middle of the academic school year. He was placed in the third grade. During his intake, not much information was gathered about his family. The clerk only noted on his documents that he was new to the community. His teachers immediately became concerned about his odd behaviors. They observed that Akiem spends a significant amount of time in the boys' bathroom every day. While in the bathroom, other students observed him flushing the toilets constantly, turning the lights on and off, and running the water in the sink continuously. The teachers and staff attributed his behavior to being mischievous and so they implemented multiple Tier I and II behavioral strategies. After two weeks of no improvement, his teachers called a meeting and the recommendation was to evaluate him for special educational services. During the evaluation, a community specialist was consulted about Akiem's behaviors. The consultant started working with Akiem and his family and started the process of gathering demographic information. Immediately the consultant learned that Akiem and his family had recently migrated from the rural areas of a developing country. He had never been exposed to electricity or bathrooms with running water. Akiem was operating out of curiosity and not out of a disability. The consultant was able to work with Akiem to help him understand the concept of plumbing and electricity. (A version of this story was shared by Dr. Omni in a 2008 workshop.)

As Akiem's story indicates, it is important to gather as much cultural and demographic information from students and families as possible. Some teachers deem this as being too inquisitive or nosy. However, it is critical in order to serve our immigrant families in a culturally responsive way.

Because of lack of information, Akiem could have been enrolled in the special educational program, which in this country boasts an overrepresentation of African American males (Moore, Henfield, and Owens 2008). Educators need to know as much as they can about their immigrant students and their families. The cost to these children and their families is too great.

Teachers can develop a questionnaire for use during initial home visits or conferences, which allows them to ask more curious, non-threatening questions about the family's cultural beliefs and practices. This can be seen as risky. However, the more comfortable the educator is with his or her own culture, the more comfortable he or she will be with gathering as much cultural information about the student as possible.

Akiem's behavior could also be compounded by the trauma of this significant transition in his life. Moving from one country to another, no matter how poor it might seem, presents a significant loss. There is loss of community, security, family, language, routine, identity, and secure attachment. These are just a few of the hidden costs of immigration for many students.

MARIE'S STORY

> On my first day of school, I sat excitedly ready to take the spelling test. I felt very proud of myself because I was not privileged to the list of words to study, but I felt pretty confident that I could master this test. The teacher read off all twenty words, and it took me no time to record my answers. I waited eagerly to get my paper back and anticipated the 100 percent that would be written across the top of the page. To my dismay, my paper read 95 percent. Whatever could have gone wrong? I knew these words. This was an easy test. I could not believe that these are the words that eight graders are learning to spell. I marched right up to the teacher and demanded that she explained why she marked an X through the word COLOUR. This is how I had been spelling it since the third grade. I knew it was correct. The teacher explained that "[t]his is the British way of spelling the word. Here in America, it is COLOR and so you got it wrong." This experience set the tone for the rest of my middle and high school career. Everything I knew to be true was not anymore.

Sometimes teachers are not aware of their power to transform a child, both positively and negatively. In the scenario above, Marie who was once a high-achieving student, bursting with ambition, became silenced by this experience. Many times, immigrant families assume the imposter syndrome. People who were once leaders in their discipline, experts in their fields, are silenced by the fact that they speak with a different accent or lack command of the formal English language of the United States of America. This also includes families who held respected jobs in their country and are now told that their degree or experience is of no value in the United States.

One of the challenges that many educational institutions face is the lack of onsite parental involvement. It is important that these educational institutions redefine parent/family involvement to include the engagement of parents and families at off campus sites. It is also important to help these students and their families learn the customs and mores so they can become active participants. Even though an immigrant family may be an English-speaking family, the pronunciation and spelling of some words, and their meanings, may be different in their home cultures.

Immigrant children face a high possibility of being bullied and ridiculed because of their language, accent, and name, even though they may speak three or four different languages. It is necessary for educators to create a safe classroom environment where these students will feel comfortable sharing, asking questions, and volunteering for tasks without becoming targets of bullying or without their participation being followed by a string of laughter or multiple requests to repeat. An appreciation for diversity is necessary for all students to feel respected and to foster growth.

CONCLUSION

> Psychology as the science of the individual was born and nourished by the philosophical foundations of individualism. We now discover the independent individual is not a universal fact, but a culture-specific belief system about the development of a person . . . it is called interdependence or collectivism. (Greenfield 1994, 3)

Over forty years ago, social psychologist Geert Hofstede studied individualism in seventy-two countries. He found that 70 percent of the countries he studied could be categorized as collectivistic, not individualistic. The United States, however, was identified as the most individualistic country in the world. An individualistic orientation conflicts with the collectivistic values that many immigrants bring from their homelands in Asia, Latin America, and parts of Africa (Zepeda, Gonzalez-Mena, Rothstein-Fisch, and Trumbull 2006).

It is important for educators to recognize that even though no one is totally individualistic or collectivistic, each person has a dominant group orientation. As schools and communities become more culturally relevant, it is important to recognize the orientation of the students or families they serve. One of the struggles that exists within the immigrant population is when the members of the older generation embrace collectivistic values, while members of second-generation immigrants and their children, particularly those who received their formal education in the United States, embrace more individualistic values.

The struggle between being an individualist or a collectivist presents a constant source of conflict between generations of immigrants, thus leading to a variety of mental health challenges including broken secure attachment. If educators are aware of these contrasting differences among immigrant students and their families, they will be more likely to respond and operate in culturally responsive ways.

When approaching immigrant families about areas of concerns with their child, it is advisable that the educator first consults with a community specialist from the child's community in order to gain perspective on how disabilities, delays, and mental health issues are viewed in this community. No parent wants to learn that there is an issue with his or her child. Therefore, these topics should be broached delicately and with cultural consideration as there is significant stigma surrounding such issues.

In some immigrant communities, accepting the fact that something is wrong with a child means accepting that the family is cursed, that there is voodoo at work against the family, or even that they have done something wrong or bad. It is also difficult for some immigrant families to accept this information because so much of the parents' dreams, goals, and aspirations is invested in the success of their child. The acceptance of depression or any other issues comes with a long-term sentence.

Many immigrant families refuse to accept that they need help, especially mental health support. When working with immigrant families and families of color, offering emotional support to help the child succeed is a more acceptable way to present one's concern rather than offering any diagnosis or using any language that could potentially pathologize the student. There are no foolproof methods or strategies for working with immigrant students and their families. The most important way to work effectively with immigrant students and families is to build authentic relationships.

Here I offer a list of simple suggestions on ways teachers can be culturally responsive when working with immigrant students and their families.

SUGGESTIONS FOR EDUCATORS WORKING WITH IMMIGRANT STUDENTS

- Be a consistent caring adult in the lives of your students. Immigrant students' lives are filled with a myriad of changes and uncertainties. The teacher's consistency will help them redevelop secure attachment, which will greatly contribute to their ability to thrive.
- Learn to pronounce a student's name properly. This can be the best relationship builder.
- Encourage students' learning so that they can have the skills and resources to make positives choices for their lives.
- Respect students/families wishes not to share information with you. They may not trust how you will use the information that you have gathered. Teachers might not realize the implications of divulging information that might initially appear to be minor.
- Understand how respect is demonstrated in your students' culture. For example, in some cultures it is insolent for a child to look their elder in the eyes. Immigrant children are often misjudged for this practice.
- Remember that common sense is only common based on common experiences. What is common to a child born in Somalia and raised in Kenya may be uncommon to a child born and raised in Laos. Teach so all students have the same foundational knowledge.
- Understand that some students are dealing with racism, sexism, or classism for the first time in their life. It is challenging for students who emigrate from countries where they operate in confidence and power to grasp the concept of oppression based on their race, socioeconomic status, or gender.
- Educate yourself on the hidden rules that your students bring with them and teach them the hidden rules of your environment. Each culture has hidden rules. These rules of operating are unwritten and seldom spoken. Knowing the hidden rule of their new environment could help immigrant students adjust and potentially prevent bullying, ridicule, and feelings of isolation.
- When working with immigrant students and their families assess for the 5 "A"s (Oni 2008):

  Availability: Inquire if the proper resources, skills, knowledge, and understanding are available to fulfill your request.

Affordability: Assess if immigrant students and their families can afford the requested materials or time. Affordability is not measured only in financial terms.

Accessibility: Inquire if immigrant students have access to resources in order to meet your requests.

Acceptability: How willing are your immigrant students and their families to accept your requests. If there is resistance, investigate the reasons.

Appropriateness: Always ask yourself if your actions or requests are appropriate and if they violate any beliefs or values.

• Look beyond what meets the eyes. See Figure 8.1, "Hidden Costs of Immigration Iceberg" (Dillard 2017). With the iceberg metaphor, often times the first thought that comes to mind is that there is more beneath the surface than anyone can see. Much like the iceberg, nine-tenths of the challenges that immigrant students and their families face are buried beneath the surface. Figure 8.1 demonstrates that only one-tenth of the cost of immigration is exposed. While the dreams, hard work, and determination are on the surface, the insurmountable losses, grief, displacement, confusion, and misplaced values lurk below. Sometimes even parents are unaware of the hidden costs of immigration for their children. Teachers can build significant relationships with immigrant students and their families that allow access to navigate down this iceberg in order to offer resources and skills to immigrant families as they navigate complex systems during transition.

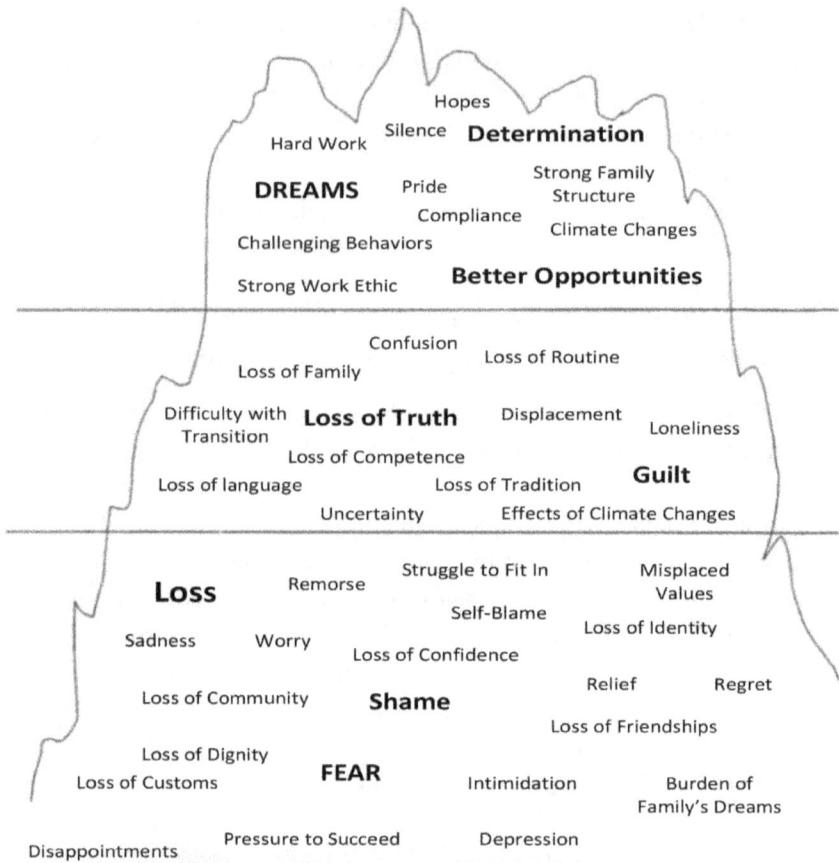

Figure 8.1.   Hidden Costs of Immigration Iceberg

REFERENCES

Dillard, A. M. 2017. "The Hidden Costs of Immigration Iceberg" [Photograph]. Robbinsdale, MN: KIP Consulting Services.

"Mental Health Facts: Children and Teens," n.d. Retrieved from https://www.nami.org/NAMI/media/NAMI-Media/Infographics/Children-MH-Facts-NAMI.pdf.

Greenfield, P. M. 1994. "Independence and Interdependence as Developmental Scripts: Implications for Theory, Research and Practice." In *Cross-Cultural Roots of Minority Child Development*, edited by P. M. Greenfield and R. R. Cocking, 1–37. Hillsdale, NJ: Lawrence Erlbaum.

Moore III, J. L., M. S. Henfield, and D. Owens. 2008. "African American Males in Special Education: Their Attitudes and Perceptions toward High School Counselors and School Counseling Services." *American Behavioral Scientist* 51 (7): 907–27.

Oni, R. 2008. "Cultural Issues Encountered in Working with African Immigrant/Refugee Children and Their Families in the Educational System." Handout. St. Cloud, MN.

Yaffe, P. 2011. "The 7% Rule Fact, Fiction, or Misunderstanding." *Ubiquity* (October 2011): 1–5. Retrieved from http://ubiquity.acm.org/article.cfm?id=2043156.

Zepeda, M., J. Gonzalez-Mena, C. Rothstein-Fisch, and E. Trumbull. 2006. *Bridging Cultures in Early Care and Education: A Training Module*. Mahwah, NJ: Lawrence Erlbaum.

Zong, J., and J. Batalova. 2017. *Frequently Requested Statistics on Immigrants and Immigration in the United States*. Washington, DC: Migration Policy Institute. Retrieved from http://www.migrationpolicy.org/article/frequently-requested-statistics-immigrants-and-immigration-united-states#ChangeOverTime.

Section III

Resources

9

IMMIGRANT AND REFUGEE RESOURCES

Mary Ellen Oslick, Marla Goins, and Shawn Anderson Brown

As teachers move to conduct classroom instruction that is responsive to students' home cultures, they must develop a knowledge base for Culturally Responsive Teaching (CRT) using detailed and factual information about those cultures (Brown 2007; Kim and Slapac 2015). According to the U.S. Department of Education, over 4.7 million foreign-born individuals are currently enrolled in pre-K to postsecondary education, which is about 6 percent of the total student population. Another 20 million students are the children of foreign-born parents.

Teachers need to have the skills and knowledge required to be effective with immigrant students and families. Milner (2011) posited that culturally relevant teachers practice this pedagogy because they believe in their students and in providing positive learning opportunities for them. The following resources have been compiled and briefly summarized to help our fellow educators begin or expand their knowledge about the diverse cultural characteristics of immigrant and refugee students and their families.

WEBSITES

Teaching Tolerance: A Project of the Southern Poverty Law Center: "New Package! Support Students from Immigrant Families," http://www .tolerance.org/blog/new-package-support-students-immigrant-families.

Teaching Tolerance is a web-based platform that contains multimedia resources for educators to construct culturally responsive classroom environments and to provide culturally responsive support to their students and families. In the spring of 2017, the staff posted a package of resources for educators to learn about immigration policies, how they affect students and their families, and how to support their students. The resources also include current events regarding immigration policies; best practices for working with English Language Learning students and families; and classroom lesson plans for engaging children in learning critically about U.S. immigration.

Facing History and Ourselves: "Global Immigration," https://www .facinghistory.org/topics/global-immigration.

Facing History and Ourselves is a nonprofit organization that provides educational resources for students and teachers to critically learn about U.S. and global systematic oppressions. In its resource library, Facing History provides a catalog of over 130 lesson plans, readings, and films for educators to engage students in learning about global immigrant, refugee experiences and identities, and immigration policies. Those resources delve into far-ranging topics on immigration in the United States and globally.

The lesson "Becoming American: Exploring Names and Identities" details activities for students to learn about the reflection of names on identity, to prelude deeper discussions about identity and immigration. Lessons contain additional resources for educators to incorporate into their preparation for the lesson, or into the lesson itself. Readings are followed by connection questions. Facing History includes links to related lessons in the films' web pages.

The Public Broadcasting Server (PBS): *Meet the New Americans*, http: //www.pbs.org/independentlens/newamericans/foreducators_index.html.

PBS provides a learning series titled *Meet the New Americans* that consists of diverse immigrant stories, including those from Nigerian, Palestinian, Dominican, Mexican, and Indian immigrants. Students read episodes that illustrate immigrants' rich, complex, and diverse experiences. The stories depict characters learning U.S. school, work, and health systems, and cultural traditions such as fast food. *Meet the New Americans* is followed by a series of interactive web pages on immigrant art, music, food, and language contributions to U.S. society. The series concludes with a quiz on immigration myths and realities.

U.S. Citizenship and Immigration Services (USCIS): "Citizenship Resource Center: Educators," https://www.uscis.gov/citizenship/teachers.

On this website, immigrants may learn about immigrant rights, naturalization, and applying for citizenship; find study materials for the civics test; and learn about local community resources and USCIS information sessions. Educators can find lesson plans, professional development materials, and training seminars for preparing immigrant adults for the civics test. Program administrators can find materials for creating adult citizenship education programs. Organizations can learn about USCIS grants for projects that service immigrant communities.

Library of Congress (LOC): "Immigration Lesson Plans," http://www.loc.gov/teachers/classroommaterials/themes/immigration/lessonplans.html.

The LOC provides online primary sources, including collections of photos, maps, citizenship documents, and texts from immigrant experiences. It also provides lesson plans on immigration for students in grades 3–12. The activities in these lessons include discussing common themes among immigrant stories; using texts to learn about French Canadian immigration to New England; and creating their own multimodal primary source archive. This web page contains access to the primary sources and lesson plans, as well as access to the LOC social media outlets.

Bridging Refugee Youth and Children's Services (BRYCS): "Immigrant/Refugee Awareness Instructional Materials," http://www.brycs.org/clearinghouse/Highlighted-Resources-Immigrant-Refugee-Awareness-Instructional-Materials.cfm.

BRYCS provides educational resources and technical training to educators and organizations that serve refugee children and families. Among its resources are online training manuals for educators, and technical consultations for organizations. BRYCS lists over twenty digital and physical resources for refugee and immigrant awareness, including curriculum guides and games that explore refugee children's experiences. Annotations of each of its recommendations, as well as information on obtaining the resources, are included.

CDF Freedom Schools: http://www.childrensdefense.org/programs/freedomschools/.

CDF Freedom Schools is a free social-justice-based literacy program for children in grades K–12. Freedom Schools sites are in thirty-one states and the U.S. Virgin Islands. They take place for six to eight weeks during summer months, although they are expanding to include yearlong sites. They provide a culturally responsive curriculum based on five core components: high-quality academic enrichment; parent and family involvement; social action and civic engagement; intergenerational servant leadership development; and nutrition, health, and mental health. Keeping with its cultural responsiveness, Freedom Schools differentiates its curriculum and instruction according to the child demographics of each site. Some sites offer bilingual instruction, in Spanish and in English.

National Education Association (NEA): "Resources for Supporting and Educating Migrant Refugee Children," http://www.nea.org/home/61723.htm.

The National Education Association (NEA) is the nation's largest professional-employee organization and commits itself to advancing the cause of public education. This web page is focused on supporting educators as they work with migrant refugee children and contains links to several of the resources already mentioned in detail (e.g., BRYCS). Several of the resources are unique to this site and include information about educating and supporting traumatized students: "Children of War: A Video for Educators" and *Educating and Supporting Traumatized Students: A Guide for School-Based Professionals.*

American Federation of Teachers: "Immigration: Protecting our Students," https://www.aft.org/our-community/immigration.

The American Federation of Teachers (AFT) is a labor union that represents teachers, paraprofessionals, and other school-related personnel. This web page contains many resources (most available in English and Spanish) for families and educators including information on Deportation Defense and a guide for educators on preparing immigrant youth and families for an ICE raid (https://www.nilc.org/wp-content/uploads/2016/06/ICE-Raids-Educators-Guide-2016-06.pdf).

One particularly helpful resource for teachers is a link to "Share My Lesson," where other educators can post lesson plans, class activities, and professional development materials. Another powerful part of the website is the addition of stories from members reporting educator and student perspectives, as well as immigration stories from Deferred Action for Childhood Arrivals (DACA) students.

Colorín Colorado: "Serving and Supporting Immigrant Students: Information for Schools," http://www.colorincolorado.org/ell-basics/serving-and-supporting-immigrant-students-information-schools.

Colorín Colorado is a national multimedia project that offers bilingual, research-based information, activities, and advice for educators and families of English-language learners (ELLs). This web page contains information that schools need to know about serving immigrant students or children of immigrants and answers to Frequently Asked Questions (FAQs). It also provides links for resources about current immigration updates (e.g., "Analyzing Trump's Immigration Ban: A Lesson Plan" from the *New York Times* and "What Do I Say to Students?" from *Teaching Tolerance*). At the bottom of the page, there are twelve links for making students feel welcome in the classroom and school.

Discovery Education: "Lesson Plan—Immigration to the United States," http://www.discoveryeducation.com/teachers/free-lesson-plans/immigration-to-the-united-states.cfm.

Discovery Education claims to be a global leader in standards-based digital content for K–12 educators, comprised of digital textbooks, multimedia content, professional development, and the largest professional learning community of its kind. The "Immigration to the United States" lesson plan explains how to deal with controversial issues that affect immigrants to the United States. It lists a number of fiction and nonfiction books about immigration that help students to formulate their own opinions. It includes links to other resources such as annotated list of literature that may be used in the classroom.

Education International: "Teachers for Migrants' and Refugees' Rights," https://www.education4refugees.org/.

Education International (EI) is the world's largest federation of unions, representing organizations of teachers and other education employees across the globe. The website promotes migrants' and refugees' rights by sharing evidence information, resources, and good practices from around the world. EI has three objectives: advocate for educational rights for all migrant and refugee children, youth, and adults; defend and promote the right to teach of migrant and refugee teachers, academics, researchers, and education support personnel; and promote education that respects diversity for open democratic, multicultural, and inclusive societies. It shares many updated news articles from around the world about immigrants and refugees, and provides a resource toolkit that includes good practices, local experiences, and resources.

Stanford Libraries: "Immigrants and Refugees in Books for Children and Young Adults," http://library.stanford.edu/guides/immigrants-and-refugees-books-children-and-young-adults.

This website is an extensive collection of children's books and young adult literature about the experiences of immigrants and refugees. It has a link for books recently received that have been published within the last two years. There are also elementary, middle school, and young adult literature sections. Unique to this resource is the inclusion of the Lexile measure. It also features a service (i.e., WorldCat) where educators can find the book at a local library.

Zinn Education Project: "BRIDGE: Popular Education Resources for Immigrant and Refugee Community Organizers," https://zinnedproject .org/materials/bridge/.

The Zinn Education Project promotes and supports the teaching of people's history in middle and high school classrooms across the country. This website offers free, downloadable lessons and articles organized by theme, time period, and reading level. The Zinn Education Project is coordinated by two nonprofit organizations: Rethinking Schools and Teaching for Change. The curriculum guide, *BRIDGE: Popular Education Resources for Immigrant and Refugee Community Organizers*, provides resources for training, leadership development, and community education.

The variety of topics covered includes the history of immigration; migration, globalization, and workers' rights; introduction to race, migration, and multiple oppression; migrant rights are human rights; LGBT rights and immigrant rights; immigrant women's leadership; building common ground with other communities: migration, race, and demographic change; and conflict transformation within community organizing.

ARTICLES AND BLOGS

University of New Mexico Latin American and Iberian Institute: "The Border: Resources for Teaching; Expanding and Enhancing Classroom Discussions of the U.S.-Mexico Border," https://resourcesfor teachingabouttheborder.wordpress.com/immigration/.

This WordPress site serves as the online accompaniment to a professional development workshop, "Teaching about the Border Using Digital Resources," that the UNM Latin American and Iberian Institute presented April 3, 2012. While some of the links have been disabled, there are still many resources available including lesson plans, visual representations, historical and economic articles, physical landscapes, and lists of narratives and literature.

Brightly: "15 Books for Kids about the Immigrant Experience in America," http://www.readbrightly.com/books-about-immigration-for-kids/.

The Brightly website was launched in partnership with Penguin Random House publishers to feature book recommendations to inspire lifelong readers. This featured blog mentions nineteen books appealing to a variety of age groups that explain through literature what it means to be a nation of immigrants. These books inspire children to think deeper about fellow Americans, their stories, and their experiences.

Pragmatic Mom: "Undocumented Immigrants in Children's Books," http://www.pragmaticmom.com/2013/07/undocumented-immigrants-in-childrens-books/; and "Modern Immigration and Refugee Experience," http://www.pragmaticmom.com/2017/05/immigration-books-kids/.

This blog, co-written by a librarian, offers extensive lists of multicultural books. Two of the lists may be of significance for those working with immigrants and refugees: "Undocumented Immigrants in Children's Books" and "Modern Immigration and the Refugee Experience." The lists include brief summaries of each book from the publishers or Amazon. These books can be used to teach empathy and compassion.

Greater Good **Magazine:** "How Teachers Can Help Immigrant Kids Feel Safe,"   http://greatergood.berkeley.edu/article/item/how_teachers_can_help_immigrant_kids_feel_safe.

The *Greater Good* magazine is published by the Greater Good Science Center (GGSC) at the University of California, Berkeley, and asserts that it "turns scientific research into stories, tips, and tools for a happier life and more compassionate society." In response to a post-election survey report of increased anxiety and fear among students, this short article offers five suggestions for supporting and educating undocumented immigrant students. One tip focuses on fostering group connectedness and belonging with circle rituals, active listening, and shared identity activities (links with examples included).

Edutopia: "Welcoming Immigrant Students into the Classroom," https://www.edutopia.org/blog/welcoming-immigrant-students-into-classroom-sara-burnett.

The George Lucas Educational Foundation was created to "identify and spread innovative, replicable, and evidence-based approaches to helping K–12 students learn better." This short blog post on the foundation's sponsored site, Edutopia, shares several best practices for establishing a welcoming classroom for immigrant students, as well as some helpful suggestions for building relationships with students and their families. The five ideas for welcoming immigrant students into the classroom can be easily implemented and modified; they also include links to other resources such as an Immigrant Timeline Scavenger Hunt and a lesson plan for creating a family history and/or digital storytelling project.

PDFS

United We Dream: "Guide for Teachers Helping DREAMers," https://unitedwedream.org/wp-content/uploads/2013/03/guide4teachers_daca.pdf.

This six-page PDF gives a brief, easy-to-read guide for teachers on how to help undocumented American youth (DREAMers) and where they can get support. The content in this guide was compiled by United We Dream from the work created by Educators for Fair Consideration

(E4FC), National Immigration Law Center (NILC), PEW Research Center, and the United States Citizenship and Immigration Services (USCIS). This resource includes a list of the top ten ways to help undocumented youth and specific steps for teachers to follow when helping DREAMers apply for DACA.

Pennsylvania Department of Education: "Supporting Undocumented, Immigrant, and Refugee Students," http://www.education.pa.gov/ Documents/K-12/SafeSchools/EquityInclusion/Resources-Supporting %20Undocumented%20and%20Immigrant%20Students.pdf.

This two-page PDF, sponsored by the Pennsylvania Department of Education, is devoted to providing information and resources for supporting undocumented, immigrant, and refugee students. This PDF has excellent resources for teachers who support immigrant children. It has articles, publications, and reports. It includes legal guidelines, models, and case studies. It also provides video interviews with actual teachers in classrooms. Lesson plans and activities are listed. Teaching tolerance is the main focus of the lesson plans and activities. It also lists other resources such as federal resources and state resources.

CONCLUSION

While this list of resources is by no means comprehensive, we hope that it can provide those working with immigrant and refugee families some support in developing a common knowledge base. These resources of services, lesson plans, documents, and children's literature can be used to promote culturally responsive teaching, culturally responsive classrooms, and culturally responsive schools.

REFERENCES

Brown, M. R. 2007. "Educating All Students: Creating Culturally Responsive Teachers, Classrooms, and Schools." *Intervention in School and Clinic* 43 (1): 57–62.

Kim, S., and A. Slapac. 2015. "Culturally Responsive, Transformative Pedagogy in the Transnational Era: Critical Perspectives." *Educational Studies* 51 (1): 17–27.

Milner, H. R. 2011. "Culturally Relevant Pedagogy in a Diverse Urban Classroom." *Urban Review* 43 (1): 66–89.

APPENDIX A

Historical Time Line of Native American Education

Table 9.1. Historical Time Line of Native American Education

Date	Period	Overview
Pre-1492	Pre-Columbian Period	Before Columbus and the invasion of Europeans, North American Indian education began at home with teaching children about cultural adherence, religion, and survival methods. Social education taught children responsibilities to their extended family, clan, band, or tribe. Vocational education taught children about domestic living off the land. Oral storytelling and ceremonies led by extended family members taught children their place in the universe.
1492–1828	Colonial Period	Treaty-based relationships were formed between the colonial governments and the various tribal entities. The Civilization Act of 1819 provided the first federal legislation to fund education for Native American children.
1828–1887	Removal, Reservation, and Treaty Period	This period was marked by the forced migration of tribes onto reservations and the creation of over 370 treaties with tribal entities relinquishing their lands for the right to self-govern. The federal government first acknowledged its responsibility of providing education to Indian students, and in 1870, Congress passed the first general appropriation for Indian schools not provided under treaties. In 1883, the first Superintendent of Indian Education was appointed to oversee the educational system for the Bureau of Indian Education (BIE) located within the Department of the Interior.

1887– 1934	Allotment and Assimilation Period	Policies created marked a shift from tribal self-governance toward the merger of Native Americans into general society. The Dawes Act of 1887 divided tribally held lands and allotted them to individual Indians and families for agricultural purposes. Tribal lands were diminished by over 90 million acres, all without compensation to the tribes. Native youth were forcibly removed from reservations and placed in boarding schools where the goal was to "Kill the Indian to Save the Man." This caused a significant disruption in the cultural and language practices of tribes. The federal government began closing reservation schools and moved toward educating Native students at public schools. By 1920, more Indian students were in public schools than BIE schools.
1934– 1945	Indian Reorganization Period	With the passing of the Indian Reorganization Act of 1934, federal policy shifted back toward an acknowledgement of tribal governments and their inherent right to self-govern. The Johnson O'Malley Act further reinforced federal accountability to ensure the specialized educational needs of Indian students were met.
1945– 1965	Termination Period	Federal policy once again shifted to renounce tribal governance and absolve the federal government of its treaties. In just two decades, over 100 tribes were terminated and more land was lost. Migration of Native children into public schools increased. In 1953, Congress enacted the Impact Aid Act, which was the first education funding provided by the Department of Education for Native American students. This act provided funding to school districts to help fund the education of children from federally impacted areas (schools located on, or near, Indian reservations that have at least 3 percent or 400 federally connected students). Impact Aid Act compensates local school districts for the education of children who reside on federal or Native-owned lands. Impact Aid funding is now part of Title VIII of the Elementary and Secondary Act, which provides a set aside for BIE schools.
1965 to current	Self- Determination Period	Despite reform efforts, the *National Study of Indian Education* in the late 1960s and the 1969 Senate subcommittee report *Indian Education: A National Tragedy, a National Challenge* documented the continued failures of Indian education. The Indian Education Act in 1972 and the Indian Self-Determination and Education Assistance Act in 1975 passed. The Indian Education Act funds special programs for Indian children on and off reservations, while the Self-Determination Act allows tribes and Indian organizations to occupy and run BIA programs, including BIE schools. The U.S. Secretary of Education's Indian Nations at Risk Task Force hearings in 1990 and 1991 indicated that many Native students still attended schools with "an unfriendly school climate

that fails to promote appropriate academic, social, cultural, and spiritual development among many Native students." The Indian Nation's Task Force documented that approximately one third of the Native student population do not graduate from high school.

The Task Force declared four national priorities: (1) Developing parent-based and culturally, linguistically, and developmentally appropriate early childhood education, (2) Making the promotion and retention of students' tribal language and culture a responsibility of the school, (3) Training more Native teachers, and (4) Strengthening tribal and Bureau of Indian Affairs colleges. In addition, they adapted the six national goals from President Bush's America 2000 program into ten national Indian education goals.

REFERENCES

Cladoosby, B. 2015. *Examining the Challenges Facing Native American Schools.* Testimony Before the House of Representatives Subcommittee on Early Childhood, Elementary, and Secondary Education: National Congress of American Indians. Retrieved from http://www.ncai.org/resources/testimony/examining-the-challenges-facing-native-american-schools.

Reyhner, J. 2006. "American Indian/Alaska Native Education: An Overview." American Indian Education. Retrieved from http://jan.ucc.nau.edu/~jar/AIE/Ind_Ed.html.

ABOUT THE EDITORS
AND CONTRIBUTORS

ABOUT THE EDITORS

Ruth McKoy Lowery, PhD, is professor of children's literature and literacy, and associate chair of the Department of Teaching and Learning at The Ohio State University. Her current research focuses on immigrant and multicultural literature, the adaptation of immigrant and at-risk students in schools, and preparing teachers to teach a diverse student population. She has published numerous articles and book chapters, and authored/coedited several books including *Immigrants in Children's Literature* (2000). She is active in the National Council of Teachers of English (NCTE), Children's Literature Assembly (CLA), and the United States Board on Books for Young People (USBBY). Her motto "*Just read*" encapsulates her love of books and belief in sharing great books with readers of all ages.

Rose M. Pringle, PhD, is associate professor in science education in the School of Teaching and Learning at the University of Florida. Her research agenda extends into two parallel, yet related research areas in science teacher education. In one line, she focuses on the development of science teachers' disciplinary content knowledge and the impact of professional development on their learning. In her other line of research, she investigates pedagogical content knowledge as a framework for shifting practices to heighten teachers' stances toward issues of social justice and their roles in positioning learners who are traditionally underrepresented in science—of special concern, the participation of girls of African descent in science and science-related careers. She therefore operates at the nexus between what knowledge teachers need and how it becomes translated into effective and culturally relevant practices that challenge assumptions and the status quo and lead to increased participation of all groups of learners in science.

Mary Ellen Oslick, PhD, is assistant professor of literacy and reading at Stetson University in DeLand, Florida. She teaches undergraduate and graduate courses in reading methods, children's literature, and critical literacy practices throughout the content areas. Her research areas of interest include social justice and critical literacy applications, multicultural children's literature, and reading and writing instruction with diverse learners. She is an active member of the International Literacy Association (ILA) and currently serves on the award selection committee for the Notable Books for a Global Society (NBGS).

ABOUT THE CONTRIBUTORS

Sara Abou Rashed has been called "an inspiration" by Children's Defense Fund founder Marian Wright Edelman. She wrote her first poem in Arabic at the age of eight and has been writing ever since. Sara's family originates from Palestine, though she was born and raised in Syria. In 2013, they moved to Columbus, Ohio, escaping the war. In 2015, just two years after learning English, Sara won the Ohio Poetry Association High School Contest and the Columbus City Poetry Slam. Her art and poetry have appeared in several publications, including the Voice of Youth Advocates and the America Library of Poetry.

Shawn Anderson Brown, PhD, is currently professor of education at Reinhardt University in the Price School of Education, where she has been a faculty member since 2003. Shawn completed her PhD at Florida State University and undergraduate degree studies at Florida A&M. Her research specialization is in English Language Learners, science, human development and differentiation. She enjoys working with preservice and in-service teachers.

Kathleen C. Colantonio-Yurko, PhD, is currently assistant professor of literacy and Literacy B-12 co-program coordinator in the Department of Education and Human Development at the College at Brockport, State University of New York. Before she became a professor, Dr. Yurko worked as a secondary English language arts teacher. In her current role, she teaches multiple undergraduate and graduate literacy and education courses. Her research interests include young adult literature, secondary ELA teaching, preservice teacher education, and topics related to adolescent literacy.

Garfield Daley is a proud husband to his wife of sixteen years and father of two teen boys. Born and raised in Jamaica, he moved to New York with his parents when he was nineteen. He moved to South Florida shortly thereafter where he lived for more than twenty years until moving to Southern California five years ago. Garfield's love and affinity for technical drawing and mechanical engineering, along with his strong work ethic form the foundation for his successes in his Audio Visual Integration career. Eclipsing his passion for his career is his love of family and his faith.

Youmna Deiri, PhD, is a postdoctoral researcher in the Department of Teaching and Learning at the Ohio State University. Her scholarship includes adolescent and community literacies, language and immigration, and women's gender and sexuality studies. Her research utilizes postcolonial and multilingual methodologies. Her dissertation on intimate literacies of belonging among women and families in Arab diasporas was informed by her being born in Saudi Arabia and growing up in Aleppo, Syria, to Syrian parents. Her teaching focuses on equity studies with preservice teachers. She has taught English as a foreign language in Turkey and Syria and English learners in the United States.

Ann M. Dillard. "You are going to America to get better opportunities." These are the words that provide constant motivation for Ann. She immigrated to the United States in 1982 at the age of thirteen. Leaving behind the familiarity of the island of Jamaica, Ann was determined to live up to the expectations of maximizing the opportunities that America has to offer, often creating her own. As a licensed marriage and family therapist, she primarily serves teens. She is the founder of KIP Consulting Service, LLC, and her nonprofit organization Project Safety Nets, serving developing communities in Senegal, West Africa.

Danling Fu, PhD, is professor in literacy, language, and culture in the College of Education at the University of Florida, where she teaches courses on language arts methods and seminars on literacy/culture and composition theory/practice. She has worked in schools and communities populated with new immigrant students and has conducted research on emergent bilingual students in New York City schools in the past three decades.

Marla Goins is a PhD candidate in the Department of Teaching and Learning at the Ohio State University. She is currently doing her dissertation in Brazil as an exchange student at the University of São Paulo. Her research explores the impact of the contemporary activism of afro-Brazilian women, on the identities and sociopolitical orientations of afro-Brazilian women preservice teachers. She teaches courses in linguistic diversity in education and equity and diversity in education in traditional and online settings. She has served the activism-based literacy program Freedom School as an intern, site coordinator, and project director.

Ivy Haoyin Hsieh, PhD, is associate professor in the Department of English Language and Culture at Tamkang Univeristy Lanyang Campus in Yilan, Taiwan. Born and raised in Taiwan, Ivy studied in the United States, receiving her PhD from the University of Florida. She taught at the Sam Houston State University before returning to her home country. Ivy has experiences living between two cultures and so is very interested in minority and immigrant issues in the world.

Cheryl Logan is a lecturer and a PhD student at the Ohio State University. She has publications in *Florida English Journal, Journal for Language Teaching*, and *Language Arts*. Her book chapters has appeared in edited volumes including *Does Non-Fiction Equate Truth?: Rethinking Disciplinary Boundaries Through Critical Literacies* (2018). Her research interests include African and African American young adult literature, and representations of Black boyhood and fatherhood. She teaches courses on diversity, multiculturalism, children's and young adult literature, and methods in language arts to undergraduates and preservice teachers.

Deandra J. McKoy is a third-grade teacher in the Alachua County School District, Florida. She earned a master of education degree from the University of Florida and is continuously seeking opportunities to cultivate her craft. Deandra facilitates a learning environment that embraces a culturally responsive pedagogy and provides meaningful and engaging standard-based learning experiences that enriches young minds. As she continues to grow as an educator, she seeks to help bridge the learning gap within her school district.

Cody Miller teaches ninth-grade English language arts at P. K. Yonge Developmental Research School, the University of Florida's affiliated K–12 laboratory school. He is also a PhD candidate in English education at the University of Florida. He can be reached at cmiller@pky.ufl.edu.

Donna Sabis-Burns, PhD, is an enrolled member of the Iroquois Six Nations and received her PhD from the University of Florida's College of Education School of Teaching and Learning. Her seminal research on Native American education has been widely cited in both social justice academic literature and national media outlets such as CBS News and *USA Today*. Presently a member of Hawaii's Department of Education, Dr. Sabis-Burns has lent her extensive experience as a researcher and leader with the U.S. Department of Education's Office of Indian Education, the U.S. Department of State's Bureau of Education and Cultural Affairs, and the District of Columbia's Office of the State Superintendent of Education.

Xiaodi Zhou, PhD, is a language and literacy education professor in the College of Education of Georgia Southwestern State University. He teaches literacy and research methods courses to preservice and in-service teachers. He has conducted research on Mexican American youths in low-income communities and writes English reading and writing series for students with diverse backgrounds.

www.ingramcontent.com/pod-product-compliance
Lightning Source LLC
Chambersburg PA
CBHW020356270326
41926CB00007B/456

* 9 7 8 1 4 7 5 8 4 7 3 9 0 *